ATLAS
OF
BRITISH HISTORY

G.S.P. FREEMAN–GRENVILLE

Cartography Lorraine Kessel

WITHDRAWN

REX COLLINGS LONDON 1979

First published by Rex Collings Ltd.
69 Marylebone High Street, London W1
& produced by Carta Ltd.

This book is available as a Hardback
and Paperback edition.

ISBN 0860 360 95 4 (Paperback)
ISBN 0860 360 94 6 (Hardback)

PREFACE

This atlas aims to provide the general reader and the student with maps of the principal themes and events in the history of the British Isles from prehistoric times until 1978. Its object is to relate their political, social and economic history to its physical setting, rivers, lowlands, hills and mountains, the nearness of the sea and the incidence of mineral wealth, which throughout this long period have been among the determinants of the country's fortunes. It would be mistaken to omit earlier times to make more space for later: Britain had already begun to exploit her mineral wealth for herself before the Romans came: in their turn they developed much of the present road system: the local government administration, radically revised in England and Wales in 1972, and in Scotland in 1973, has pre-Norman bases, some of which survive: the system of royal courts, developed as assizes under the Plantagenets, was revised only in 1973: the same physical system determined the siting of towns, castles and monasteries as determined the industrial revolution and the growth of later industry. The discovery of gas and oil in the sea expands that pattern. One cannot treat the fortunes of the British Isles geographically or historically without reference to Europe, to the former Empire or to the present Commonwealth, or to wars, whether European or global, in which the country has been engaged.

It is necessary to remark especially on maps 3 to 6, which show the state of knowledge of prehistory as it was early in 1976. The exceptional drought of that summer revealed no less than 600 hitherto unrecorded prehistoric sites in Scotland, and more in England. It will of course be some time before so many sites can be accurately assessed or dated.

I forebear to mention all those to whom I owe a debt of gratitude for advice or assistance: they have my warmest thanks, and will, I am sure, forgive the omission of what would be far too long a catalogue of names.

Sheriff Hutton
York

G.S.P.F.–G.

CONTENTS

1. THE BRITISH ISLES ACCORDING TO CLAUDIUS PTOLEMY C. 150

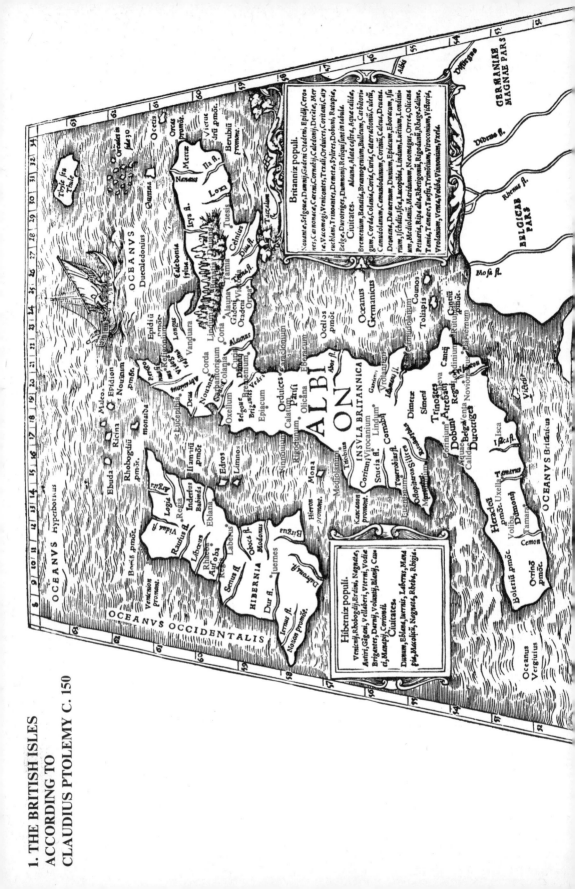

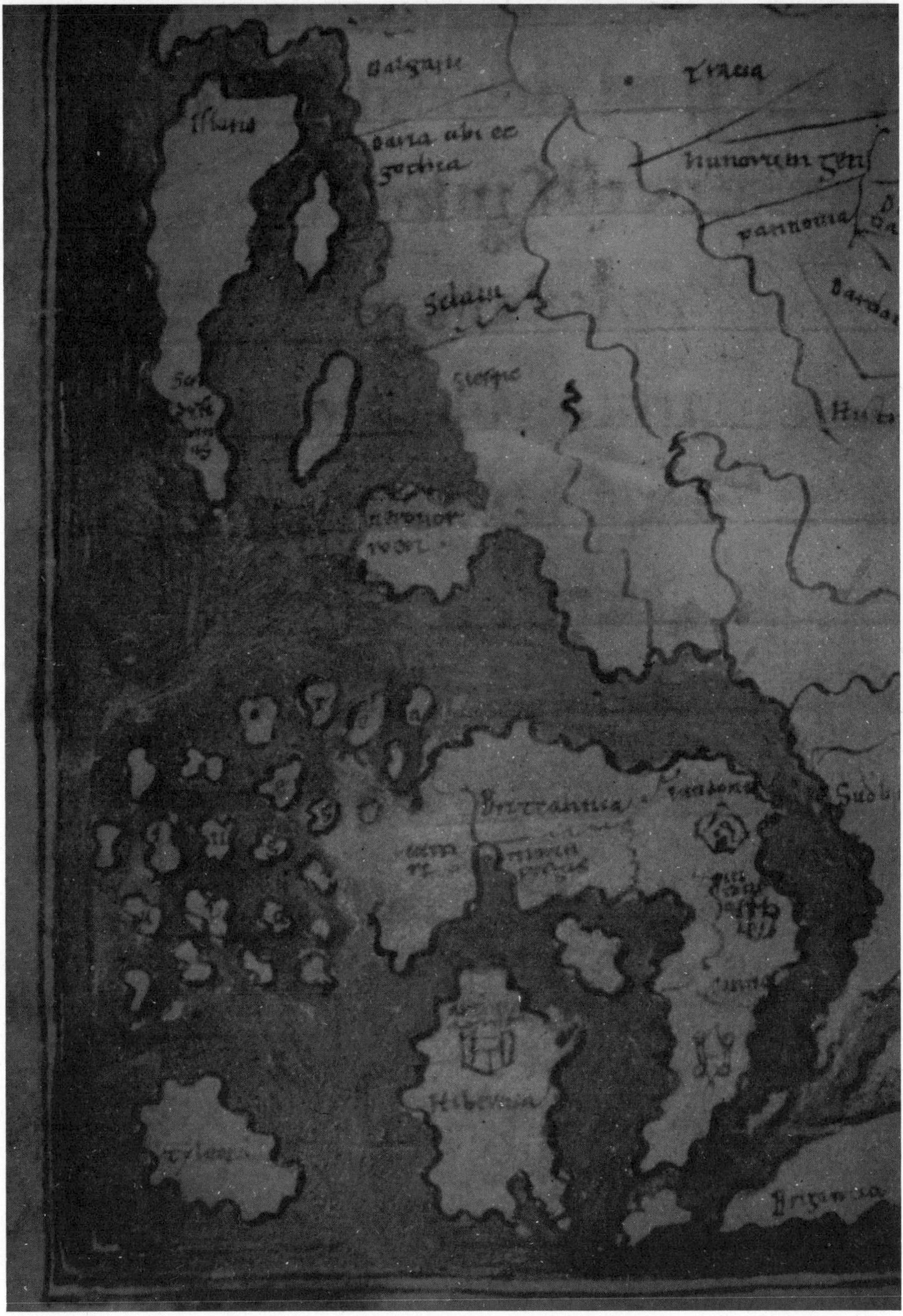

2. THE BRITISH ISLES IN ALFRED'S EDITION OF OROSIUS

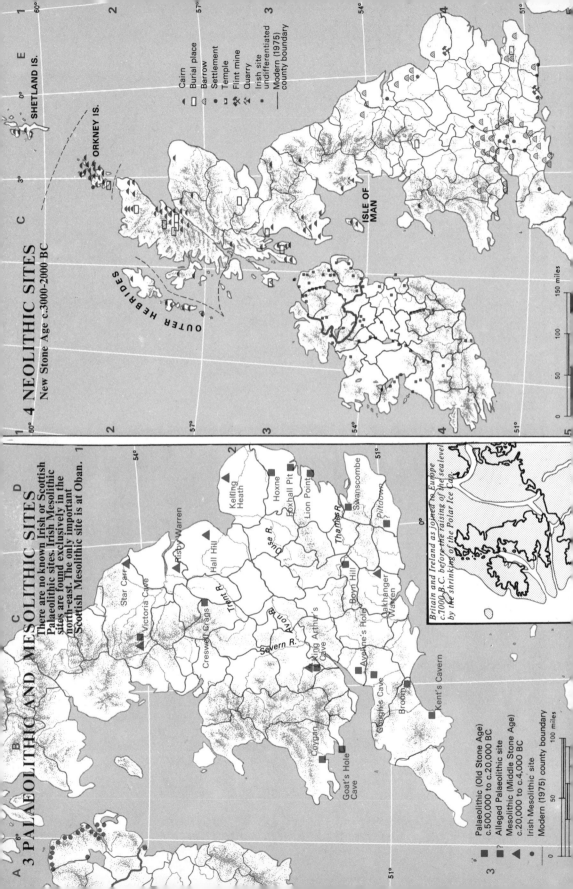

4 NEOLITHIC SITES
New Stone Age c.3000–2000 BC

Legend:
- ◢ Cairn
- ▭ Burial place
- △ Barrow
- ● Settlement
- ⋈ Temple
- ✕ Flint mine
- ✕ Quarry
- ▪ Irish site undifferentiated
- —— Modern (1975) county boundary

SHETLAND IS.

ORKNEY IS.

OUTER HEBRIDES

ISLE OF MAN

0   50   100   150 miles

3 PALAEOLITHIC AND MESOLITHIC SITES

There are no known Irish or Scottish Palaeolithic sites. Irish Mesolithic sites are found exclusively in the north-east. The only important Scottish Mesolithic site is at Oban.

Star Carr

Risby Warren

Victoria Cave

Kelling Heath

Hall Hill

Ouse R.

Hoxne

Foxhall Pit

Creswell Crags

Lion Point

Trent R.

Thames R.

Swanscombe

Avon R.

Pildown ?

King Arthur's Cave

Boyn Hill

Severn R.

Oakhanger Warren

Aveline's Hole

Paviland Goat's Hole Cave

Gough's Cave

Broom

Kent's Cavern

Britain and Ireland as joined to Europe c.7000 B.C. before the raising of the sea level by the shrinking of the Polar Ice Cap.

Legend:
- ■ Palaeolithic (Old Stone Age) c.500,000 to c.20,000 BC
- ■ Alleged Palaeolithic site
- ▲ Mesolithic (Middle Stone Age) c.20,000 to c.4,000 BC
- ● Irish Mesolithic site
- —— Modern (1975) county boundary

0   50   100 miles

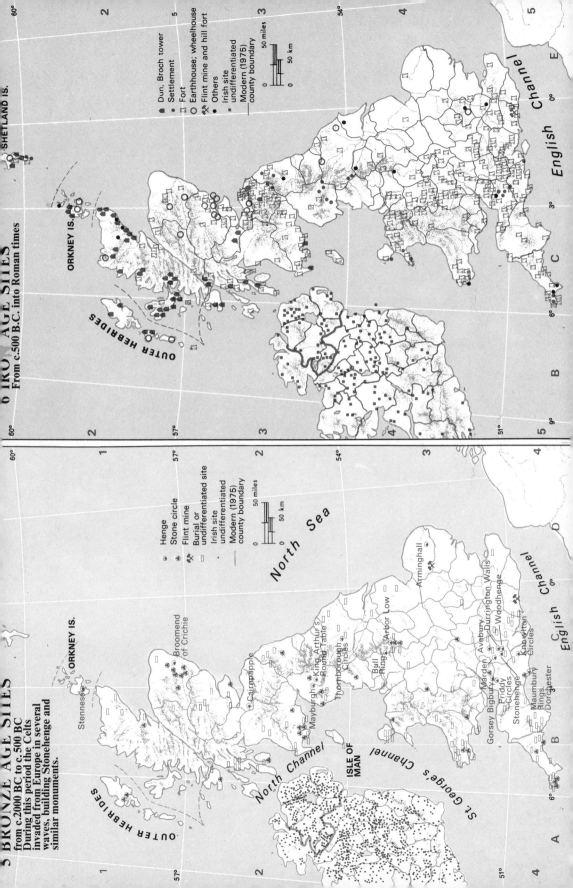

6 IRON AGE SITES
From c.500 B.C. into Roman times

Legend:
- Dun, Broch tower
- Settlement
- Fort
- Earthhouse; wheelhouse
- Flint mine and hill fort
- Others
- Irish site undifferentiated
- Modern (1975) county boundary

50 miles
50 km

SHETLAND IS.

ORKNEY IS.

OUTER HEBRIDES

English Channel

5 BRONZE AGE SITES
from c.2000 BC to c.500 BC
During this period the Celts invaded from Europe in several waves, building Stonehenge and similar monuments.

Legend:
- Henge
- Stone circle
- Flint mine
- Burial or undifferentiated site
- Irish site undifferentiated
- Modern (1975) county boundary

50 miles
50 km

North Sea

ORKNEY IS.

OUTER HEBRIDES

Stennes

Cairnpapple

Broomend of Crichie

Mayburgh
King Arthur's Round Table
Thornborough Circles
Arbor Low
Bull Ring
Marden
Priddy Circles
Gorsey Bigbury
Avebury
Durrington Walls
Woodhenge
Knowlton Circles
Maumbury Rings
Stonehenge
Dorchester

Arminghall

North Channel

ISLE OF MAN

St. George's Channel

English Channel

8 THE ROMAN CONQUEST OF BRITAIN
AD 43 until the division into two provinces, AD 197

7 JULIUS CAESAR'S CAMPAIGNS IN BRITAIN
55 BC and 54 BC

ENGLAND

- Wheathampstead
- *CATUVELLAUNI*
- Londinium London
- *CANTII*
- North Downs
- *CANTII*
- Durovernum Canterbury
- Deal
- Stour R.
- Cantium Prom. South Foreland
- Dubris Dover

Channel

FRANCE
- Ambleteuse
- Bolonia Boulogne

→ 55 BC campaign
→ 54 BC campaign
✕ Battle
▲ Base camp
CANTII Celtic tribe

0   25 miles
0   25 km

0°   2°

CALEDONES
VACOMAGI
VENICONES

Pinnata Castra
Inchtuthil

Horrea Classis
Carpow

EPIDII

139-42, Wall of Antoninus Pius built; abandoned c.184

VOTADINI

AD 83-84

Trimontium
Newstead

122, Hadrian's Wall begun; 196/97, destroyed; 205-08 rebuilt.

SELGOVAE

NOVANTAE

Arbela
South Shields

Luguvalium
Carlisle

Corstopitum
Corbridge

83-84, Agricola conquers northern Britain as far as Scottish Lowlands; defeats Caledonians at Mons Graupius, position unknown. Supporting fleet circum—navigates Britain

Cataractonium
Catterick

BRIGANTES

Derventio
Malton

PARISI

71, York built as Legionary fortress

Eburacum
York

61, Mona attacked; 78, Mona and N. Wales finally conquered.

Humber R.

Danum
Doncaster

Mona
Anglesey

Deva
Chester

Mamucium
Manchester

Lindum
Lincoln

Segontium
Caernarvon

DECEANGLI

AD 61

Midlands

AD 43

CORNOVII

Trent R.

AD 47

61, Iceni under Boudicca (Boadicea) sack London; revolt suppressed.

ICENI

ORDOVICES

Viriconium
Cornoviorum
Wroxeter

47-51, P. Ostorius Scapula's campaign in Wales; 48, midlands disarmed; 51, Caratacus rebels and is defeated.

Severn

CORITANI

Ratae
Coritanorum
Leicester

Venonae
High Cross

Venta Icenorum
Caistor

Isurium
Brigantum
Aldborough

Durolipons
Cambridge

DEMETAE

SILURES

AD 46

Glevum
Gloucester

Corinium
Dobunorum
Cirencester

TRINOVANTES

Verulamium
St Albans

Camulodunum
Colchester

CATUVELLAUNI

Venta Silurum
Caerwent

DOBUNI

Aquae Sulis
Bath

AD 43

Thames

Calleva
Atrebatum
Silchester

Londinium
London

CANTII

Regulbium
Reculver

Rutupiae
Richborough

Durovernum
Canterbury

Dubris
Dover

BELGAE

ATREBATES

Venta Belgarum
Winchester

REGNI

Regnum
Chichester

Lemanis
Lympne

Lindinis
Ilchester

DUROTRIGES

Durnovaria
Dorchester

Isca
Dumnoniorum
Exeter

Vectis Insula
Is. of Wight

DUMNONII

Conquest under Aulus Plautus and Emperor Claudius AD 43: campaign in the midlands, east and under future Emperor Vespasian as far as Exeter before 47, campaigns as far as Venonae (High Cross) and to Lindum (Lincoln) and the Humber

✛ Military fort town
• Colonia

211 Britain divided into two provinces, military north of the boundary, civil south of it

■ Former tribal capital

ICENI Celtic tribe

▬▬▬ Roads, some previously existing tracks, developed over a period

0   25   50 miles
0   25   50 km

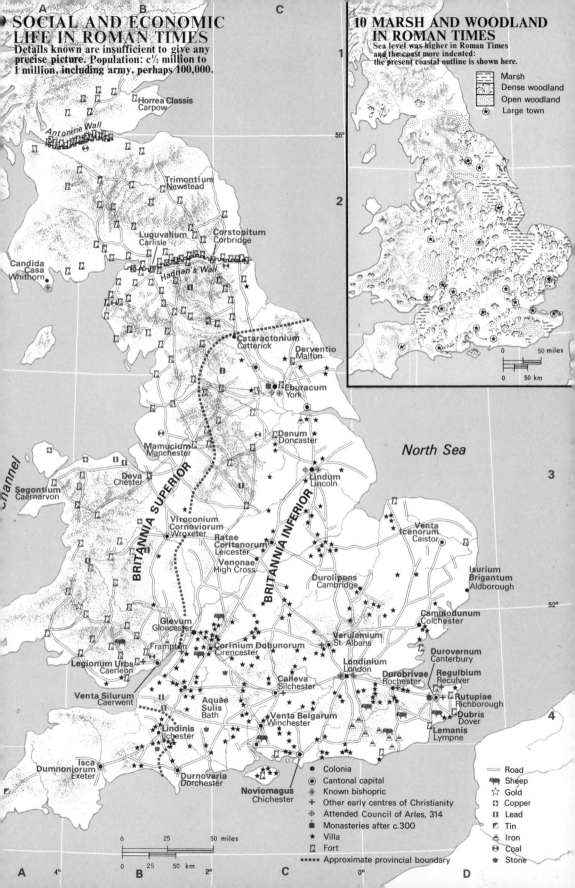

SOCIAL AND ECONOMIC LIFE IN ROMAN TIMES

Details known are insufficient to give any precise picture. Population: c½ million to 1 million, including army, perhaps 100,000.

10 MARSH AND WOODLAND IN ROMAN TIMES

Sea level was higher in Roman Times and the coast more indented: the present coastal outline is shown here.

- Marsh
- Dense woodland
- Open woodland
- ⊛ Large town

Legend (main map):
- ● Colonia
- ◉ Cantonal capital
- ⊕ Known bishopric
- ✚ Other early centres of Christianity
- ⊕ Attended Council of Arles, 314
- ■ Monasteries after c.300
- ★ Villa
- ⌂ Fort
- ▪▪▪ Approximate provincial boundary

- ═ Road
- Sheep
- ☆ Gold
- ⌂ Copper
- Lead
- Tin
- △ Iron
- Coal
- ✦ Stone

Horrea Classis
Carpow

Antonine Wall

Trimontium
Newstead

Luguvalium
Carlisle

Corstopitum
Corbridge

Candida
Casa
Whithorn

Hadrian's Wall

Cataractonium
Catterick

Derventio
Malton

Eburacum
York

Danum
Doncaster

Mamucium
Manchester

Lindum
Lincoln

Deva
Chester

Segontium
Caernarvon

BRITANNIA SUPERIOR

Viroconium
Cornoviorum
Wroxeter

Ratae
Coritanorum
Leicester

Venonae
High Cross

Venta
Icenorum
Caistor

Durolipons
Cambridge

Isurium
Brigantum
Aldborough

BRITANNIA INFERIOR

Glevum
Gloucester

Camulodunum
Colchester

Verulamium
St. Albans

Frampton

Corinium Dobunorum
Cirencester

Legionum Urbs
Caerleon

Durovernum
Canterbury

Londinium
London

Durobrivae
Rochester

Regulbium
Reculver

Venta Silurum
Caerwent

Aquae
Sulis
Bath

Calleva
Silchester

Rutupiae
Richborough

Venta Belgarum
Winchester

Dubris
Dover

Lindinis
Ilchester

Lemanis
Lympne

Isca
Dumnoniorum
Exeter

Durnovaria
Dorchester

Noviomagus
Chichester

North Sea

Channel

55°
52°

0   25   50 miles
0   25   50 km

0   50 miles
0   50 km

A   B   C   D
4°   2°   0°

11 BRITAIN AND ITS INVADERS, 4TH TO 5TH CENTURIES

287–94. Carausius usurps Britain:
294–96. Allectus murders Carausius and usurps Britain.
296 Constantius Chlorus recovers Britain. York and Chester rebuilt.
Britain divided into four provinces, boundaries not known. Hadrian's Wall rebuilt against the Picts.
306 Constantius dies at York: succ. Constantine the Great.
406 Usurper Constantine III withdraws troops from Britain:
410 Honorius informs British that they are responsible for their own safety.

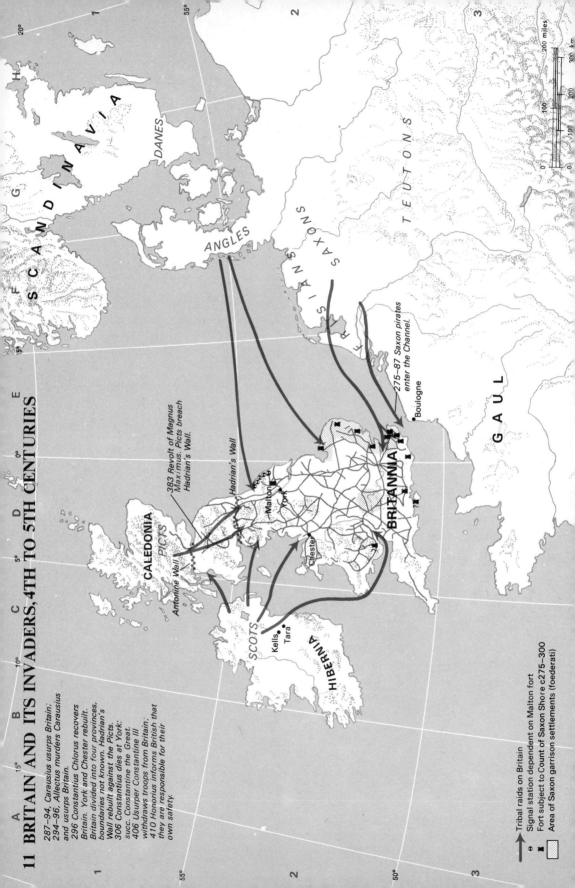

383 Revolt of Magnus Maximus. Picts breach Hadrian's Wall.

275–87 Saxon pirates enter the Channel.

SCANDINAVIA

DANES

ANGLES

FRISIANS

SAXONS

TEUTONS

GAUL

Boulogne

CALEDONIA

PICTS

Antonine Wall

Hadrian's Wall

Malton

York

Chester

BRITANNIA

HIBERNIA

SCOTS

Kells
Tara

Tribal raids on Britain
Signal station dependent on Malton fort
Fort subject to Count of Saxon Shore c275–300
Area of Saxon garrison settlements (foederati)

200 miles
300 km

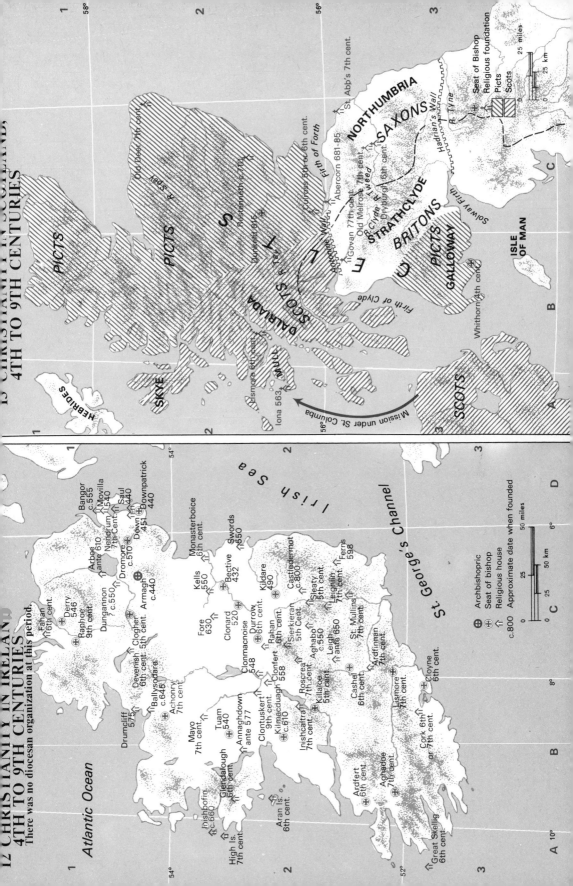

13 CHRISTIANITY IN SCOTLAND, 4TH TO 9TH CENTURIES

12 CHRISTIANITY IN IRELAND 4TH TO 9TH CENTURIES
There was no diocesan organization at this period.

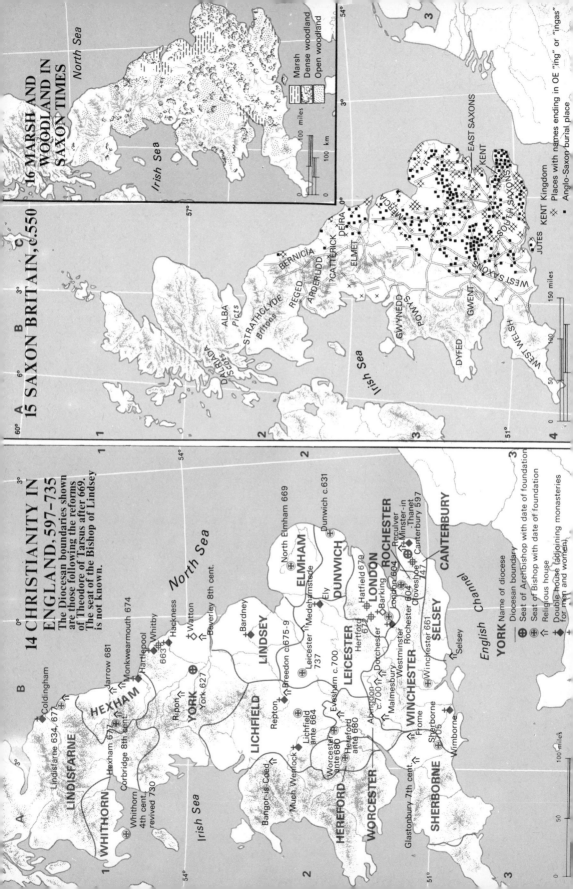

14 CHRISTIANITY IN ENGLAND, 597–735

15 SAXON BRITAIN, c.550

16 MARSH AND WOODLAND IN SAXON TIMES

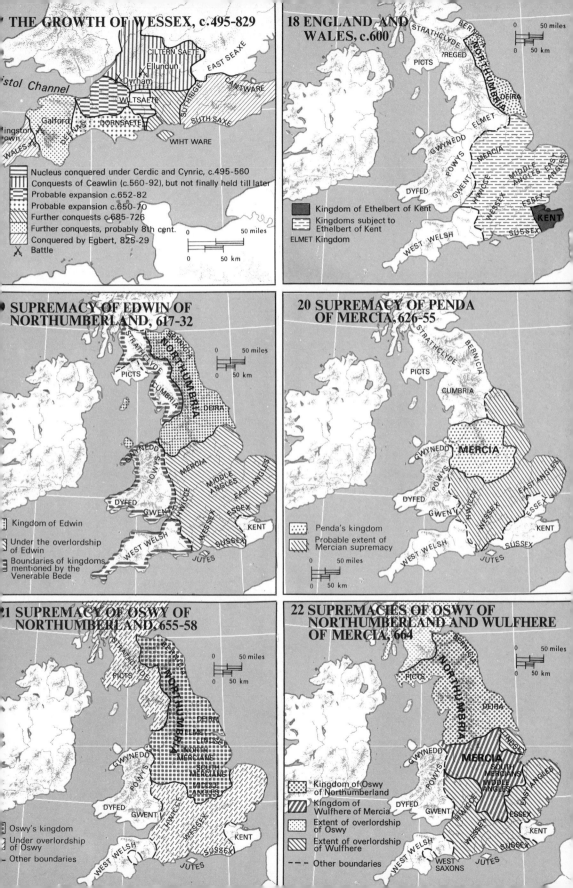

THE GROWTH OF WESSEX, c.495-829

CILTERN SAETE
Ellundun
Dyrham
WILTSAETE
EAST SEAXE
CANTWARE
SUTHRIGE
SUTH SAXE
istol Channel
Galford
ingston
own
DEFNAS
DORNSAETE
WALES
WIHT WARE

Nucleus conquered under Cerdic and Cynric, c.495-560
Conquests of Ceawlin (c.560-92), but not finally held till later
Probable expansion c.652-82
Probable expansion c.650-70
Further conquests c.685-726
Further conquests, probably 8th cent.
Conquered by Egbert, 825-29
X Battle

0   50 miles
0   50 km

18 ENGLAND AND WALES, c.600

0   50 miles
0   50 km
STRATHCLYDE
?REGED
BERNICIA
NORTHUMBRIA
PICTS
DEIRA
ELMET
GWYNEDD
POWYS
MERCIA
MIDDLE EAST
ANGLES ANGLES
DYFED
GWENT
HWICCE
WESSEX
ESSEX
KENT
WEST WELSH
SUSSEX

Kingdom of Ethelbert of Kent
Kingdoms subject to Ethelbert of Kent
ELMET Kingdom

SUPREMACY OF EDWIN OF NORTHUMBERLAND, 617-32

0   50 miles
0   50 km
BERNICIA
NORTHUMBRIA
STRATHCLYDE
PICTS
CUMBRIA
DEIRA
GWYNEDD
POWYS
MERCIA
MIDDLE
ANGLES
DYFED
EAST ANGLES
GWENT
HWICCE
WESSEX ESSEX
WEST WELSH
SUSSEX
KENT
JUTES

Kingdom of Edwin
Under the overlordship of Edwin
Boundaries of kingdoms mentioned by the Venerable Bede

20 SUPREMACY OF PENDA OF MERCIA, 626-55

STRATHCLYDE
BERNICIA
PICTS
CUMBRIA
GWYNEDD
MERCIA
POWYS
DYFED
EAST ANGLES
GWENT
HWICCE
WESSEX
ESSEX
KENT
WEST WELSH
SUSSEX
JUTES

Penda's kingdom
Probable extent of Mercian supremacy

0   50 miles
0   50 km

21 SUPREMACY OF OSWY OF NORTHUMBERLAND, 655-58

0   50 miles
0   50 km
STRATHCLYDE
PICTS
NORTHUMBRIA
DEIRA
ELMET
LINDSEY
NORTH MERCIANS
GWYNEDD
POWYS
SOUTH MERCIANS
MIDDLE ANGLES
DYFED
HWICCE
WESSEX
GWENT
WEST WELSH
KENT
SUSSEX
JUTES

Oswy's kingdom
Under overlordship of Oswy
Other boundaries

22 SUPREMACIES OF OSWY OF NORTHUMBERLAND AND WULFHERE OF MERCIA, 664

0   50 miles
0   50 km
BERNICIA
NORTHUMBRIA
PICTS
DEIRA
LINDSEY
MERCIA
SOUTH MERCIANS
MIDDLE ANGLES
GWYNEDD
POWYS
EAST ANGLES
HWICCE
GWENT
WESSEX
ESSEX
WEST WELSH
WEST SAXONS
SUSSEX
KENT
JUTES

Kingdom of Oswy of Northumberland
Kingdom of Wulfhere of Mercia
Extent of overlordship of Oswy
Extent of overlordship of Wulfhere
- - - Other boundaries

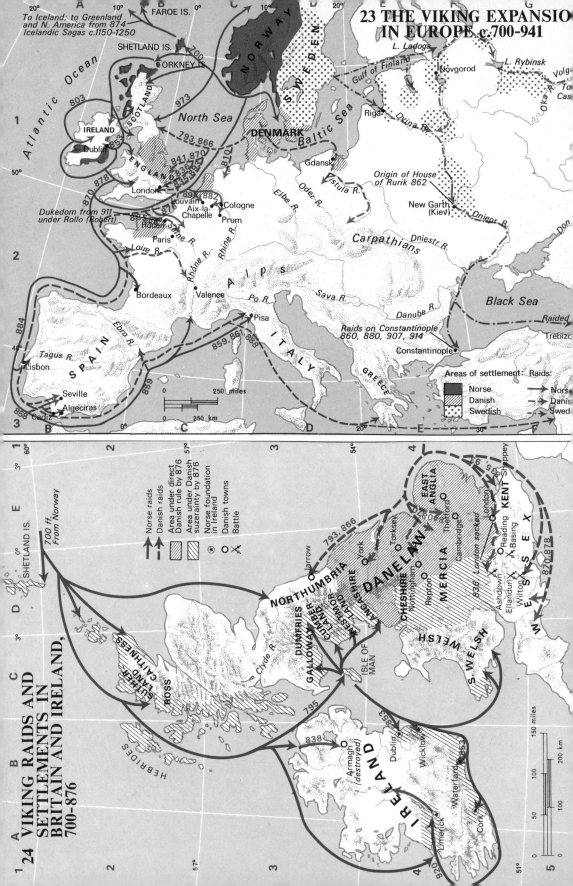

23 THE VIKING EXPANSION IN EUROPE c. 700-941

To Iceland; to Greenland and N. America from 874 Icelandic Sagas c. 1150-1250

FAROE IS.

SHETLAND IS.

ORKNEY IS.

NORWAY

SWEDEN

L. Ladoga

L. Rybinsk

Novgorod

Gulf of Finland

Volga

To Cas

Atlantic Ocean

North Sea

Baltic Sea

DENMARK

Riga

Dvina R.

Oka R.

IRELAND

SCOTLAND

Dublin

ENGLAND

Gdansk

Origin of House of Rurik 862

New Garth (Kiev)

London

Louvain

Aix-la-Chapelle

Cologne

Prum

Oder R.

Vistula R.

Elbe R.

Dnepr R.

Rouen

Paris

Seine R.

Rhine R.

Carpathians

Don

Dukedom from 911 under Rollo (Robert)

Loire R.

Dniestr R.

Rhône R.

Alps

Bordeaux

Valence

Po R.

Sava R.

Danube R.

Black Sea

Pisa

Raided

Ebro R.

Raids on Constantinople 860, 880, 907, 914

Trebizo

SPAIN

Tagus R.

ITALY

Constantinople

Lisbon

GREECE

Seville

Algeciras

250 miles

Gadiz

250 km

Areas of settlement:

Norse
Danish
Swedish

Raids:

Nors
Danis
Swed

---

24 VIKING RAIDS AND SETTLEMENTS IN BRITAIN AND IRELAND, 700-876

700 ff. From Norway

SHETLAND IS.

Norse raids
Danish raids
Area under direct Danish rule by 876
Area under Danish suzerainty by 876
Norse foundation in Ireland
Danish towns
Battle

SUTHERLAND CAITHNESS

ROSS

HEBRIDES

NORTHUMBRIA

Jarrow

York

CUMBERLAND

WESTMORLAND

DANELAW

EAST ANGLIA

Thetford

KENT

Sheppey

DUMFRIES

GALLOWAY

Clyde R.

LANCASHIRE

CHESHIRE

Torksey

Nottingham

MERCIA

Cambridge

London

London sacked

Reading

ESSEX

ISLE OF MAN

Repton

836

Ashdown

Ellandun

Wilton

Basing

S. WELSH

N. WELSH

795

WESSEX

838

IRELAND

Armagh (destroyed)

Dublin

Wicklow

Limerick

Waterford

Cork

150 miles

200 km

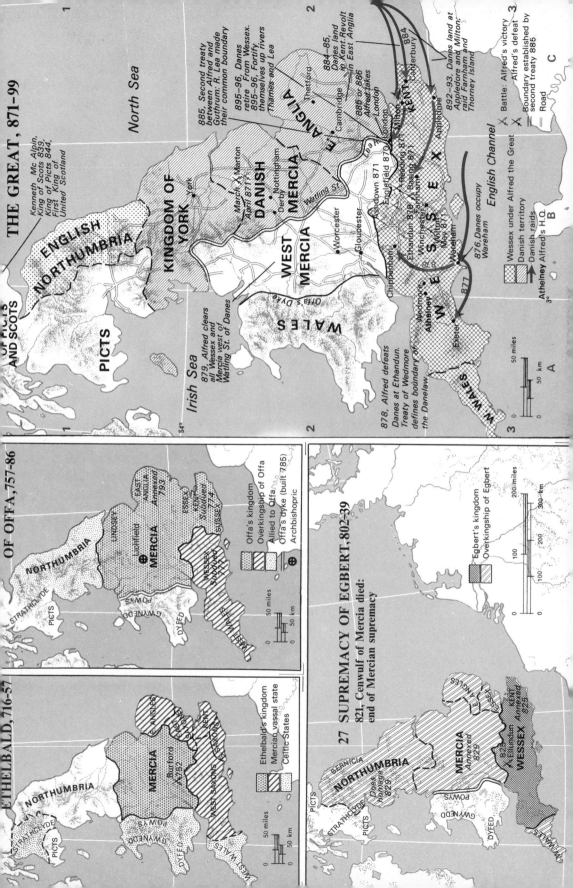

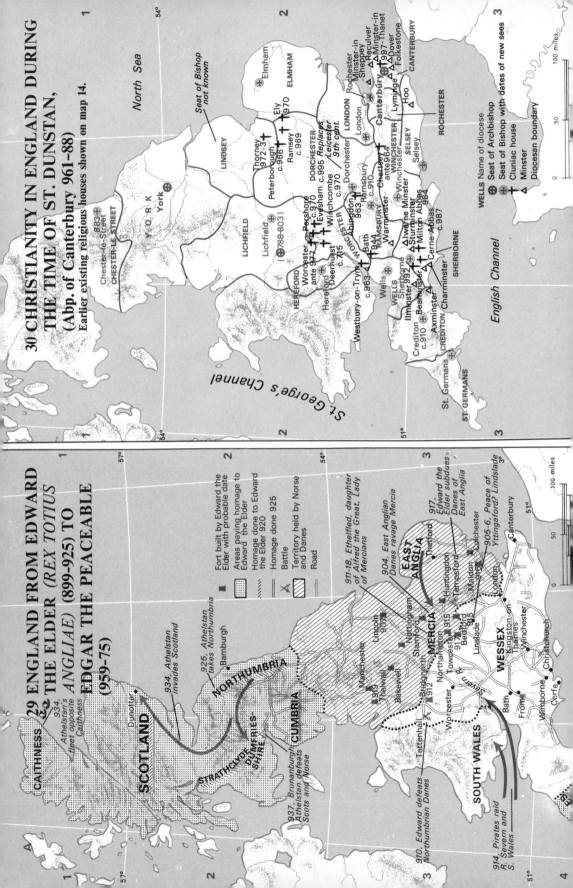

30 CHRISTIANITY IN ENGLAND DURING THE TIME OF ST. DUNSTAN, (Abp. of Canterbury 961-88)

Earlier existing religious houses shown on map 14.

North Sea

Seat of Bishop not known

Y·O·R·K York
Chester-le-Street CHESTER-LE-STREET 883
LINDSEY
Elmham ELMHAM
LICHFIELD Lichfield 788-803
Thorney 972-3 Ely 970
Peterborough c.966 Ramsey 969
Pershore c.970 Evesham c.970 Leicester *Replaces* 9th cent.
Worcester ante 977 Dorchester Dorchester c.970 LONDON London
WORCESTER Abingdon 963 Ramsey Rochester -in-Sheppey Minster-in-Thanet
Hereford Deerhurst Chertsey ante 964 Reculver Canterbury Minster-in-Thanet 997
HEREFORD c.715 DORCHESTER Bath c.910 WINCHESTER Winchester Lyminge Dover Folkestone
Westbury-on-Trym c.963 944 Warminster SELSEY Selsey Hoo CANTERBURY
Wells Milton Abbas 964 ROCHESTER
WELLS Sherborne Ilminster 992 Sturminster c.970
Crediton c.910 Beaminster Cerne Abbas c.987
Axminster SHERBORNE
CREDITON Charminster
St. Germans ST. GERMANS

English Channel
St George's Channel

WELLS Name of diocese
⊕ Seat of Archbishop
✚ Seat of Bishop with dates of new sees
△ Cluniac house
✚ Minster
Diocesan boundary

29 ENGLAND FROM EDWARD THE ELDER (*REX TOTIUS ANGLIAE*) (899-925) TO EDGAR THE PEACEABLE (959-75)

934, Athelstan's fleet opposite Caithness
934, Athelstan invades Scotland
925, Athelstan takes Northumbria

CAITHNESS
SCOTLAND Dunottar
Bamburgh
NORTHUMBRIA
STRATHCLYDE DUMFRIESSHIRE CUMBRIA
937, Brunanburgh? Athelstan defeats Scots and Norse
910, Edward defeats Northumbrian Danes

Manchester
Thelwall 919
Bakewell Chester
Bridgnorth 912
Tettenhall Lincoln 907
Stamford Nottingham Stamford
Derby Leicester
MERCIA Northampton Towcester 917
Worcester Bedford 917
Severn R. Tamworth 913
911-18, Ethelfled, daughter of Alfred the Great, Lady of Mercians
904, East Anglian Danes ravage Mercia
Thetford EAST ANGLIA
917, Edward the Elder subdues Danes of East Anglia
Huntingdon Tempsford
Colchester
Maldon 915
WESSEX London
Bath Frome Kingston-on-Thames Canterbury
Wimborne Winchester
Corfe Christchurch
SOUTH WALES
914, Pirates raid R. Severn and S. Wales
905-6, Peace of Yttingaford? Lindslade

Fort built by Edward with probable date
Areas paying homage to Edward the Elder
Homage done to Edward the Elder 920
Homage done 925
Battle
Territory held by Norse and Danes
Road

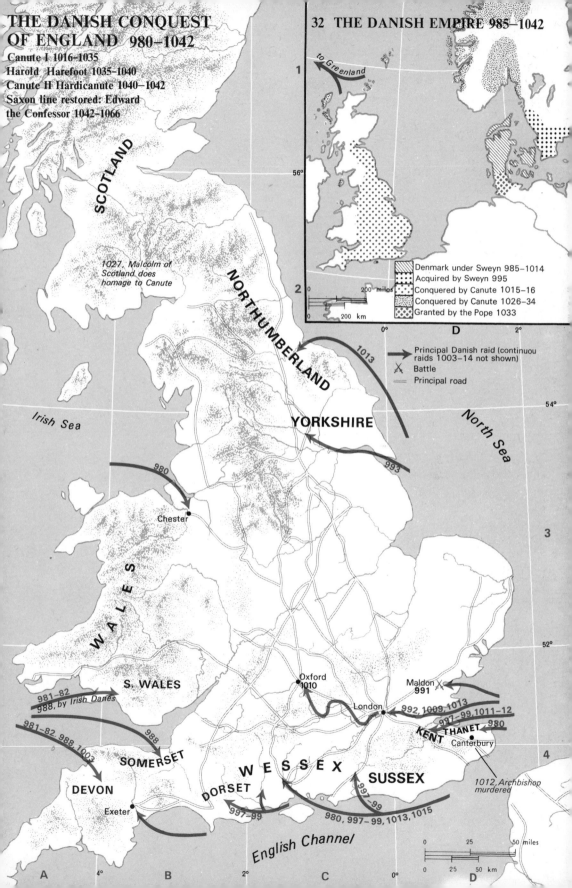

THE DANISH CONQUEST OF ENGLAND 980–1042

Canute I 1016–1035
Harold Harefoot 1035–1040
Canute II Hardicanute 1040–1042
Saxon line restored: Edward
the Confessor 1042–1066

32 THE DANISH EMPIRE 985–1042

to Greenland

▨	Denmark under Sweyn 985–1014
▦	Acquired by Sweyn 995
⠿	Conquered by Canute 1015–16
▨	Conquered by Canute 1026–34
⊠	Granted by the Pope 1033

→ Principal Danish raid (continuou raids 1003–14 not shown)
✕ Battle
═ Principal road

SCOTLAND

1027, Malcolm of
Scotland does
homage to Canute

NORTHUMBERLAND

1013

YORKSHIRE

993

Irish Sea

North Sea

980

Chester

W A L E S

S. WALES

981–82, by Irish Danes
988

981–82. 988. 1003

SOMERSET

988

Oxford
1010

Maldon ✕
991

London
992, 1009, 1013

997–99, 1011–12

980

KENT
THANET

Canterbury

1012, Archbishop
murdered

DEVON

Exeter

DORSET

W E S S E X

997–99

SUSSEX

997–99

980, 997–99, 1013, 1015

English Channel

56°

54°

52°

0   200 miles
0   200 km

0   25   50 miles
0   25   50 km

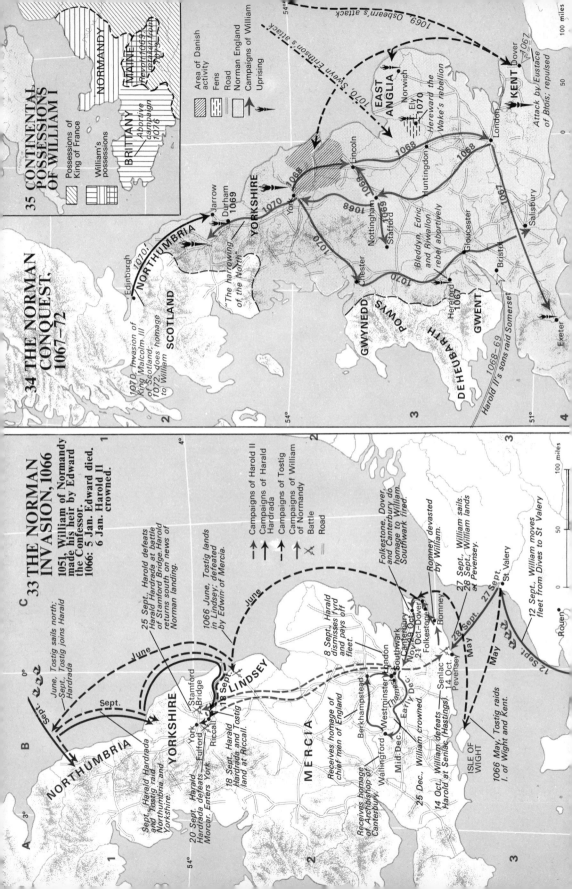

33 THE NORMAN INVASION, 1066

34 THE NORMAN CONQUEST, 1067–72

35 CONTINENTAL POSSESSIONS OF WILLIAM I

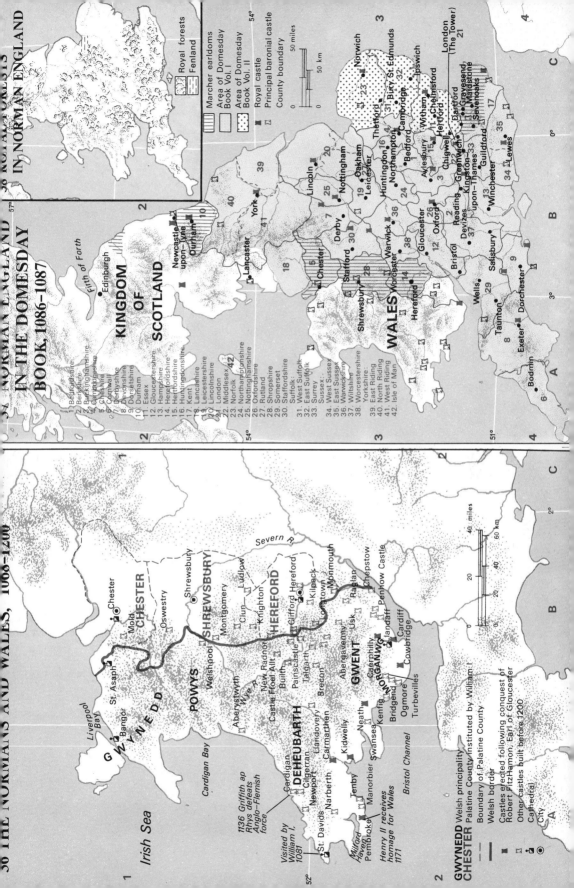

30 THE NORMANS AND WALES, 1086–1200

Irish Sea

Liverpool Bay

GWYNEDD

GWY

Bangor

St. Asaph

Mold

Chester ◉⚔

CHESTER

Oswestry

Severn R.

Shrewsbury ●

SHREWSBURY

POWYS

Welshpool

Montgomery

Clun

Ludlow

Aberystwyth

Knighton

New Radnor

Castle Foel Allt

Wye R.

Builth

HEREFORD

Clifford

Hereford ◉⚔

Kilpeck

Cardigan Bay

DEHEUBARTH

Cardigan

Cilgerran

1136 Griffith ap
Rhys defeats
Anglo-Flemish
force

Llandovery

Talgarth

Brecon

Painscastle

Longtown

Monmouth

Abergavenny

Usk

Raglan

Chepstow

Penhow Castle

*Visited by
William I,
1081*

St. David's

Newport

Narberth

Tenby

Manorbier

Pembroke

Milford Haven

Carmarthen

Kidwelly

Swansea

Neath

Kenfig

Ogmore

Bridgend

Turbevilles

GWENT

Caerphilly

Llandaff

Cardiff

Cowbridge

MORGANWG

Bristol Channel

*Henry II receives
homage for Wales
1171*

GWYNEDD Welsh principality
CHESTER Palatine County instituted by William I

– – – Boundary of Palatine County

──── Welsh border

⚔ Castles erected following conquest of
Robert FitzHamon, Earl of Gloucester

⚔ Other castles built before 1200

◉ Cathedral

⦿ City

40 miles
60 km
20
40
20

---

32 NORMAN ENGLAND IN THE DOMESDAY BOOK, 1086–1087

30 ROYAL GUESTS IN NORMAN ENGLAND

Firth of Forth

Edinburgh

KINGDOM

OF

SCOTLAND

Newcastle-upon-Tyne

Durham ⚔ 10

York ⚔ 41

Lancaster ⚔ 18

Chester 5

Derby 7

Nottingham 25

Lincoln 20

Stafford 28

Shrewsbury

Warwick 38

Worcester 14

Hereford

Gloucester 12

WALES

Oxford 26

Leicester 19

Rutland 27

Northampton 24

Huntingdon 16

Cambridge 4

Bedford 3

Bury St. Edmunds

Thetford

Norwich 23

Ipswich

Aylesbury 2

Hertford 15

Chigwell

Witham

Chelmsford 31 32

London (The Tower) 21

Greenwich

Kingston-upon-Thames 33

Dartford

Gravesend

Maidstone

Sevenoaks 17

Guildford

Winchester 13

Lewes 35

Reading

Devizes 37

Bristol

Wells

Salisbury 9

Taunton 29

Dorchester

Exeter 6

Bodmin

Marcher earldoms

Area of Domesday Book Vol. I

Area of Domesday Book Vol. II

⚔ Royal castle

⚔ Principal baronial castle

County boundary

Royal forests

Fenland

1 Bedfordshire
2 Berkshire
3 Buckinghamshire
4 Cambridgeshire
5 Cheshire
6 Cornwall
7 Derbyshire
8 Devonshire
9 Dorsetshire
10 Durham
11 Essex
12 Gloucestershire
13 Hampshire
14 Herefordshire
15 Hertfordshire
16 Huntingdonshire
17 Kent
18 Lancashire
19 Leicestershire
20 Lincolnshire
21 London
22 Middlesex
23 Norfolk
24 Northamptonshire
25 Nottinghamshire
26 Oxfordshire
27 Rutland
28 Shropshire
29 Somerset
30 Staffordshire
31 West Suffolk
32 East Suffolk
33 Surrey
34 West Sussex
35 East Sussex
36 Warwickshire
37 Wiltshire
38 Worcestershire
39 East Riding
40 North Riding
41 West Riding
42 Isle of Man

50 miles
50 km

39 THE CHURCH IN BRITAIN, c. 1090–1150

1066: 35 religious houses
1100: 50 abbeys, 29 cells
and 45 alien priories

North Sea

Legend:

— Diocesan boundaries after the reforms of Lanfranc (1070–89)
⊕ Archbishopric
■ Cathedral city
⊕ Councils held by Lanfranc, with date
▤ New cathedral
◇ New abbey
⌒ New priory
⌢ Gilbertines
✳ Savigni
⊤ White Canons
✤ Cluny
★ Celtic foundations existing in or after 1050

Fortrose
Elgin
Monymusk
Brechin
Dunkeld
Inchaffray
Monifieth
Dunblane
Abernethy
Iona
Muthill
St. Andrews
Leven
Inchcolm
Newhouse

Alnwick

From Chester-le-Street 994

Whithorn
Carlisle 1133
Durham
From Chester-le-Street 994

Calder
Byland
Jervaulx
Malton
Rushen Furness
York
Watton

From Lichfield 1075 Removed to Coventry 1102
From Dorchester
Alvingham
Sixhills
Basingwerk Chester
Bullington
Lincoln
Kirkstead
Combermere
Newstead Cattley
Swineshead
Buildwas Haverholme
Sempringham
Norwich
From Thetford
Ely 1109
From Thetford
Coventry
Bury St. Edmunds
Hereford
Worcester
Chicksand
St. Albans
Coggeshall
Stratford Langthorne
Neath
Gloucester 1081,1085
London 1075, 1078 (Westminster Hall)
Rochester
Stanley
From Wells 1080 Bath
Chicksand
Winchester 1072, 1076
Canterbury (St. Augustine's)
Old Sarum
Lewes
Battle
From Crediton 1050
Exeter
Chichester
From Selsey 1075
Quarr
Buckfast
From Sherborne 1075

Irish Sea

IRELAND

English Channel

0   50   100 miles
0 50 100 150 km

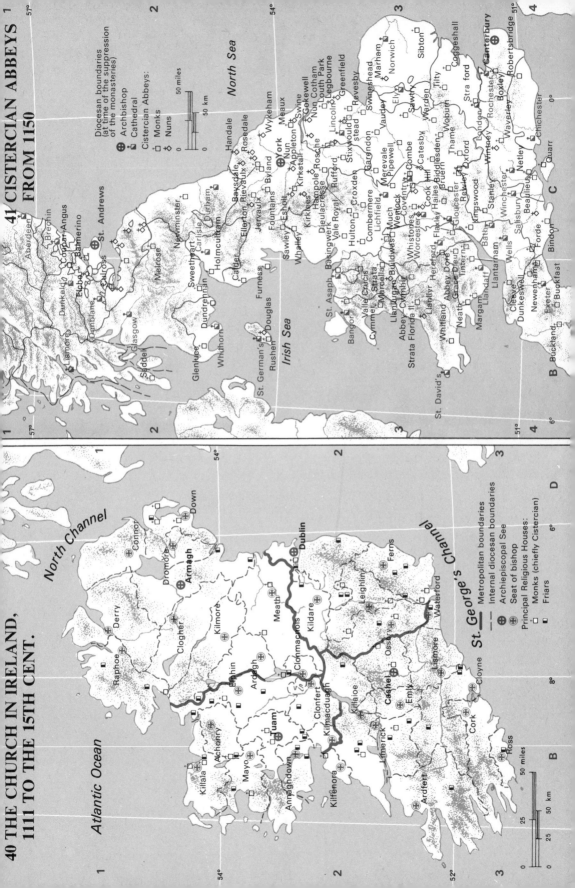

40 THE CHURCH IN IRELAND, 1111 TO THE 15TH CENT.

41 CISTERCIAN ABBEYS FROM 1150

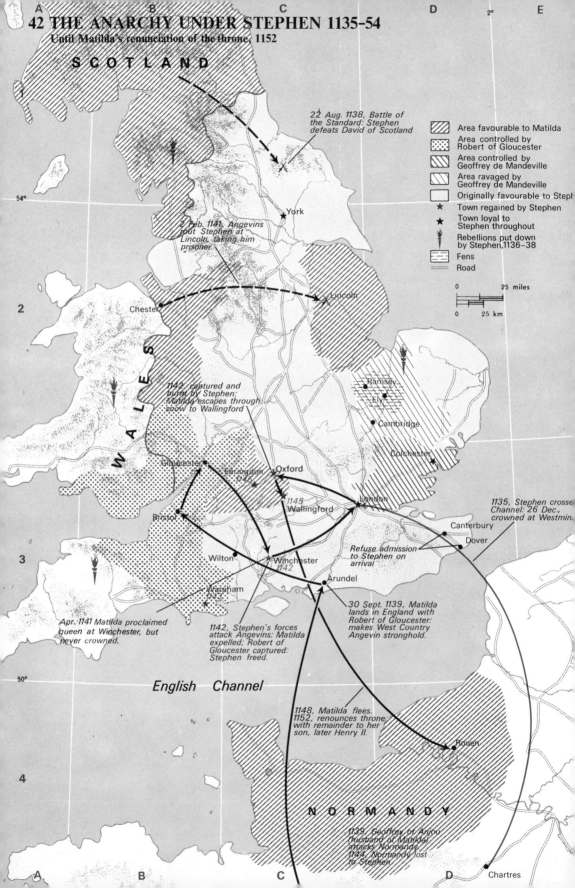

42 THE ANARCHY UNDER STEPHEN 1135-54
Until Matilda's renunciation of the throne, 1152

SCOTLAND

22 Aug. 1138, Battle of
the Standard: Stephen
defeats David of Scotland

York

Area favourable to Matilda

Area controlled by
Robert of Gloucester

Area controlled by
Geoffrey de Mandeville

Area ravaged by
Geoffrey de Mandeville

Originally favourable to Steph

★ Town regained by Stephen

★ Town loyal to
Stephen throughout

Rebellions put down
by Stephen,1136–38

Fens

Road

2 Feb. 1141, Angevins
rout Stephen at
Lincoln, taking him
prisoner

0   25 miles
0   25 km

Chester

Lincoln

Ramsey
Ely
Cambridge

1142 captured and
burnt by Stephen:
Matilda escapes through
snow to Wallingford

Colchester

W A L E S

Gloucester
Farringdon
1145
Oxford
1145
Wallingford

London

1135, Stephen crosse
Channel: 26 Dec.,
crowned at Westmin

Bristol

Canterbury
Dover

Wilton
Winchester
1142

Refuse admission
to Stephen on
arrival

Arundel

Apr. 1141 Matilda proclaimed
queen at Winchester, but
never crowned.

Wareham
1143

1142, Stephen's forces
attack Angevins: Matilda
expelled; Robert of
Gloucester captured:
Stephen freed.

30 Sept. 1139, Matilda
lands in England with
Robert of Gloucester:
makes West Country
Angevin stronghold.

English   Channel

1148, Matilda flees.
1152, renounces throne
with remainder to her
son, later Henry II.

Rouen

54°

50°

N O R M A N D Y

1139, Geoffrey of Anjou
(husband of Matilda)
attacks Normandy:
1144, Normandy lost
to Stephen.

Chartres

43 THE DOMINIONS OF HENRY II PLANTAGENET. 1154–89

First Plantagenet King.
In popular legend this family
was descended from the Devil

Henry's dominions:

- By cession from his father, 1149
- By succession from his father, 1150
- Dukedoms in the right of his wife, 1152
- By succession in the right of his mother, 1154
- Lands over which Henry claimed suzerainty
- Possessions of King of France
- Vassal dukedom

SCOTLAND

North Sea

IRELAND

Dublin

GWYNEDD

ENGLAND

WALES

1167–71, Invasions
by Henry II or his
vassals

29 Dec. 1170,
St. Thomas Becket
murdered

London

Canterbury

Winchester

Nov. 1153, Stephen
agrees to share
power with Henry

English Channel

1174, William the Lion.
King of Scots, does
homage to Henry
for Scotland

NORMANDY

Paris

Falaise

MAINE

BRITTANY

FRANCE

ANJOU

Atlantic Ocean

HOLY ROMAN EMPIRE

POITOU

BURGUNDY

AQUITAINE

AUVERGNE

Bordeaux

0   50   100   150 miles

0   100   200 km

TOULOUSE

GASCONY

SPAIN

Mediterranean
Sea

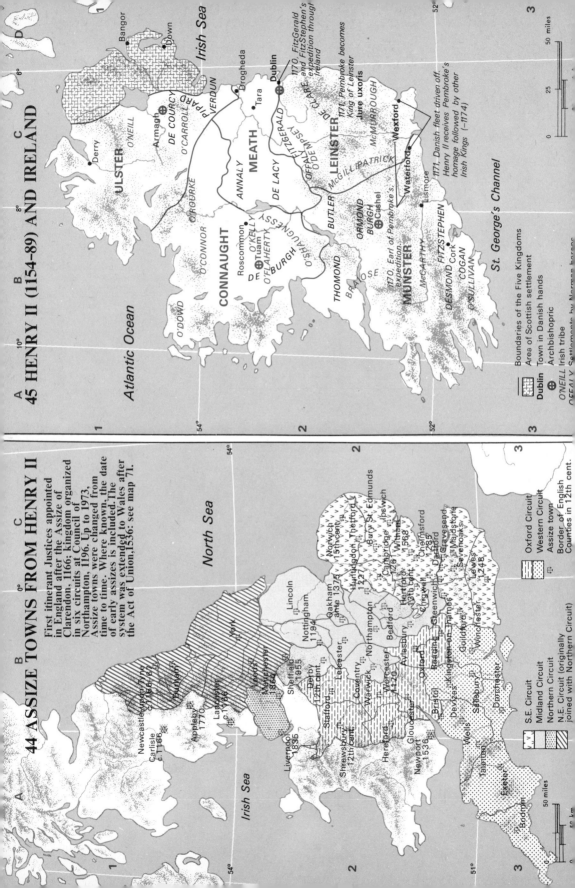

45 HENRY II (1154–89) AND IRELAND

44 ASSIZE TOWNS FROM HENRY II

First itinerant Justices appointed in England after the Assize of Clarendon, 1166; kingdom organized in six circuits at Council of Northampton, 1176. Up to 1973, Assize towns were changed from time to time. Where known, the date of early assizes is included. The system was extended to Wales after the Act of Union, 1536: see map 71.

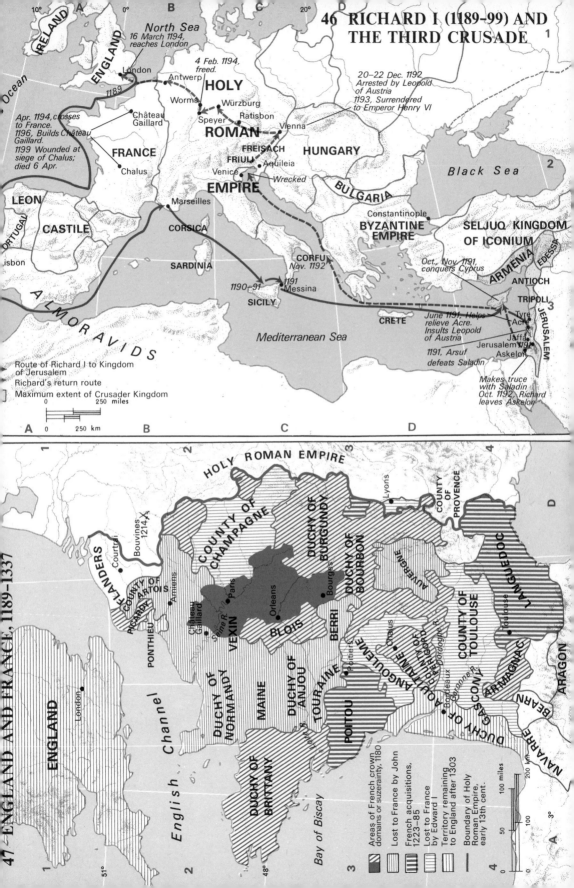

46 RICHARD I (1189-99) AND THE THIRD CRUSADE

North Sea

16 March 1194, reaches London

4 Feb. 1194, freed.

London

Antwerp

HOLY

Worms   Würzburg

Speyer   Ratisbon

ROMAN

20-22 Dec. 1192 Arrested by Leopold of Austria 1193, Surrendered to Emperor Henry VI

Vienna

Château Gaillard

Apr. 1194, crosses to France. 1196, Builds Château Gaillard. 1199 Wounded at siege of Chalus; died 6 Apr.

FRANCE

Chalus

EMPIRE

FREISACH

FRIULI   Aquileia

Venice   *Wrecked*

HUNGARY

Black Sea

BULGARIA

LEON

CASTILE

Marseilles

CORSICA

SARDINIA

Constantinople

BYZANTINE EMPIRE

SELJUQ KINGDOM OF ICONIUM

ARMENIA   EDESSA

CORFU *Nov. 1192*

Oct, Nov 1191 conquers Cyprus

ANTIOCH

TRIPOLI

JERUSALEM

1190-91   1191 Messina

SICILY

CRETE

Tyre

Acre

June 1191, Helps relieve Acre. Insults Leopold of Austria

Jaffa

Jerusalem 1192

Askelon

1191, Arsuf defeats Saladin

Mediterranean Sea

Makes truce with Saladin Oct. 1192. Richard leaves Askelon

A L M O R A V I D S

Route of Richard I to Kingdom of Jerusalem

Richard's return route

Maximum extent of Crusader Kingdom

0   250 miles

0   250 km

HOLY ROMAN EMPIRE

Lyons

COUNTY OF PROVENCE

Bouvines 1214

Courtrai

FLANDERS

COUNTY OF ARTOIS

PICARDY

PONTHIEU

COUNTY OF CHAMPAGNE

DUCHY OF BURGUNDY

DUCHY OF BOURBON

Bourges

AUVERGNE

LANGUEDOC

ENGLAND

London

English Channel

Château Gaillard

VEXIN

Paris

Orleans

BLOIS

BERRI

Chalus

COUNTY OF TOULOUSE

Toulouse

ARMAGNAC

ARAGON

DUCHY OF NORMANDY

MAINE

DUCHY OF ANJOU

TOURAINE

POITOU

Poitiers

ANGOULEME

DUCHY OF AQUITAINE

Bordeaux

DUCHY OF GASCONY

BEARN

NAVARRE

DUCHY OF BRITTANY

Bay of Biscay

Areas of French crown domains or suzerainty, 1180

Lost to France by John

French acquisitions, 1223-85

Lost to France by Edward I

Territory remaining to England after 1303

Boundary of Holy Roman Empire, early 13th cent.

50   100 miles

100   200 km

48 ECONOMIC AND SOCIAL LIFE, 1200–1300

49 ROYAL FORESTS IN THE 13TH CENTURY

Royal forests

Tay R.

Clyde R.

Southern Uplands

Nith R.

Tweed R.

Cheviot Hills

Esk R.

Tyne R.

Tees R.

Swale R.

Whitby

Rievaulx

Jervaulx

Byland

Ure R.

Furness

Fountains

Wharfe R.

York

Beverley

Kirkstall

Ribble R.

Hull

Ouse R.

Irish Sea

North Sea

Aire R.

Bolton

Pennine Chain

Mersey R.

Lincoln

Weaver R.

Principal weaving centr

Monastery supplying w

Cinque port

Town with Jewish quar

Road

Dee R.

Dove R.

Trent R.

Nottingham

Lynn

Yare R.

W A L E S

Severn R.

Leicester

Stamford

Crowland

Norwich

Cambrian Mountains

Buildwas

Welland R.

Waveney R.

Ouse R.

Coventry

Huntingdon

Bury
St. Edmunds

Worcester

Warwick

Northampton

Cambridge

Ipswich

Avon R.

Bedford

Wye R.

Winchcombe

Sudbury

Towy R.

Dore

Gloucester

Cotswold Hills

Oxford

Lea R.

Colchester

Neath

Chiltern Hills

Hertford

Tintern

Wallingford

London

Bristol

Avon R.

Marlborough

Thames R.

North

Canterbury

Mendip Hills

Devizes

Wey R.

Downs

Sandwich

Exmoor

Parrett R.

Wilton

Waverley

Medway R.

Dover

Exe R.

Salisbury

Winchester

The Weald

Rye

Avon R.

Test R.

Hastings

Romney

Stour R.

Itchen R.

Arun R.

Winchelsea

Tamar R.

Dartmoor

Beaulieu

Buckfastleigh

English Channel

0   25   50 mile

0   25   50 km

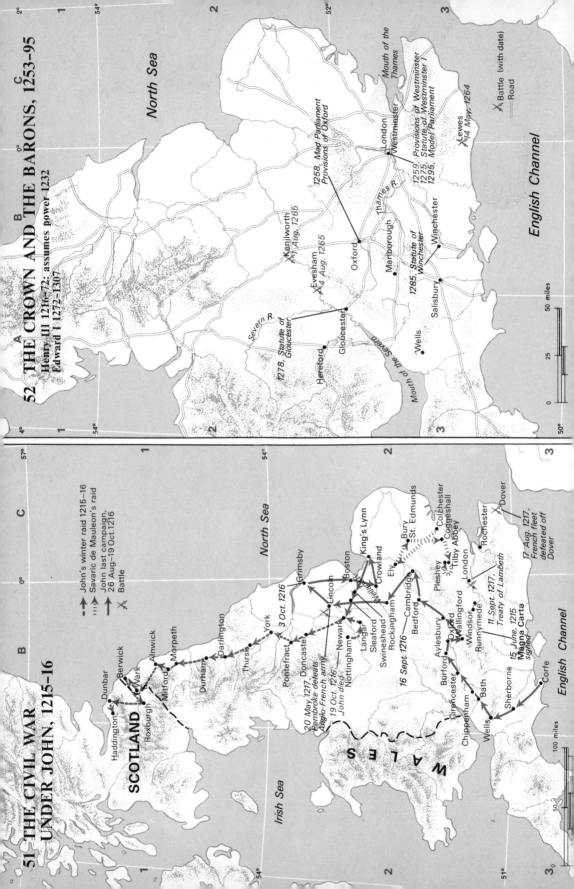

52 THE CROWN AND THE BARONS, 1253–95

Henry III 1216–72: assumes power 1232
Edward I 1272–1307

North Sea

Mouth of the Thames

1258, Mad Parliament
Provisions of Oxford

Kenilworth
×1 Aug. 1265

Evesham
×4 Aug. 1265

Oxford

Marlborough

Severn R.

1278, Statute of
Gloucester

Hereford

Gloucester

Mouth of the Severn

Thames R.

London
Westminster

1259, Provisions of Westminster
1275, Statute of Westminster I
1295, Model Parliament

Lewes
×14 May, 1264

Winchester

1285, Statute of
Winchester

Salisbury

Wells

English Channel

× Battle (with date)
— Road

0   25   50 miles

51 THE CIVIL WAR UNDER JOHN, 1215–16

- ▪— John's winter raid 1215–16
- ····▸ Savaric de Mauleon's raid
- ➤ John last campaign,
  26 Aug.–19 Oct. 1216
- × Battle

SCOTLAND

North Sea

Haddington

Dunbar

Berwick

Roxburgh

Wark

Alnwick

Mitford

Morpeth

Durham

Darlington

Thirsk

Grimsby

Boston

King's Lynn

Crowland

Ely

Bury
St. Edmunds

Colchester

Coggeshall
Tilby Abbey

Pleshey

London

York
3 Oct. 1216

Pontefract

Doncaster

20 May 1217
Pembroke defeats
Anglo-French army

Newark
John died
19 Oct. 1216

Nottingham

Lincoln

Langar

Sleaford

Swineshead

Rockingham

16 Sept 1216

Cambridge

Bedford

Aylesbury

Oxford
Wallingford

Windsor

Runnymede

11. Sept. 1217,
Treaty of Lambeth

Rochester

Dover

17 Aug. 1217,
French fleet
defeated off
Dover

Burford

Cirencester

Bath

Sherborne

15 June, 1215
Magna Carta
signed

Chippenham

Wells

Corfe

WALES

Irish Sea

English Channel

0   50   100 miles

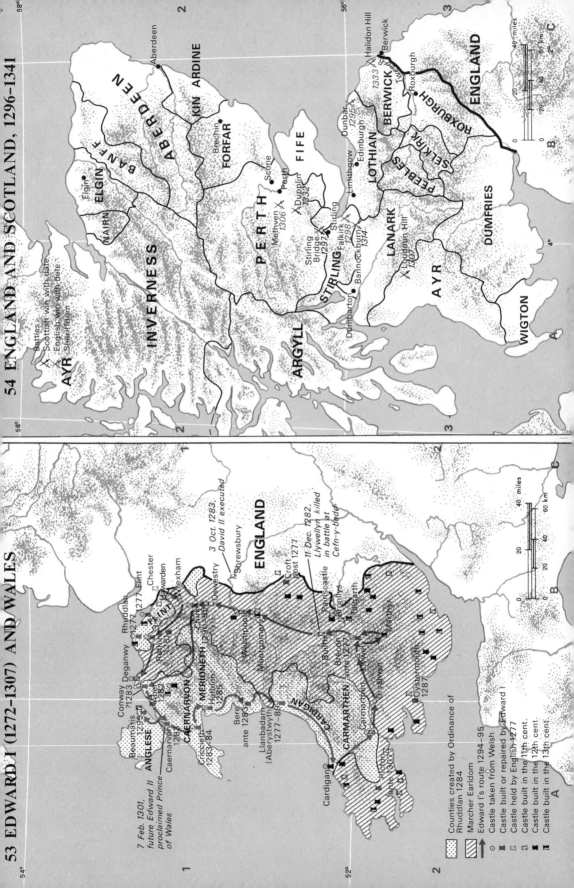

54 ENGLAND AND SCOTLAND, 1296–1341

53 EDWARD I (1272–1307) AND WALES

55 ECONOMIC AND SOCIAL LIFE, 1300-140[0]

North Sea

Southern Uplands

Clyde R.
Nith R.
Tweed R.
Esk R.

Cheviot Hills

Newcastle
Carlisle
Hartlepool
Tyne R.
Guisborough
Tees R.
Richmond
Swale R.
Scarborough
Ure R.
Ripon
Lancaster
Ribble R.
Wharfe R.
Bridlington
Beverley
York
Halifax
Hull
Aire R.
Ouse R.

Irish Sea

Bangor
Mersey R.
Doncaster
Derwent R.
Lincoln
Caernarvon
Chester
Weaver R.
Idle R.
Boston
Cambrian Mountains
Dee R.
Derby
Dove R.
Spalding
Stafford
Trent R.
Grantham
Stamford
Shrewsbury
Lichfield
Leicester
Lynn
Norwich
Severn R.
—B
north
Welland R.
Yare R.
Yarmouth
Wye R.
Coventry
Huntingdon
Waveney R.
Cardigan
Towy R.
Hereford
Worcester
Northampton
Bury St. Edmunds
St. Davids
Daventry
Cambridge
Sudbury
Ipswich
Haverfordwest
Brecon
Gloucester
Northleach
Ouse R.
Hadleigh
Colchester
Avon R.
Ware
Coggeshall
Oxford
St. Albans
Chiltern Hills
Lea
Bristol
Reading
London
Thames R.
Avon R.
Kennet
Sandwich
Bridgwater
Mendip Hills
Guildford
North Downs
Canterbury
Exmoor
Salisbury
Winchester
Wey
Hythe
Wey R.
Shaftesbury
Southampton
Arun R.
Medway
The Weald
Dover
Romney
Chichester
Lewes
Rye
Winchelsea
Hastings
Test R.
Stour R.
Exeter
Exe R.
Tamar R.
Dartmoor

English Channel

56°
52°
50°
4°

Scale:
0 25 50 miles
0 25 50 km

Legend

York	Principal town
⊕	Principal port
⊕	Cinque port
✦	Centre of wool-industry
═	Road
☯	Coal
▲	Iron
▯	Lead and silver
▯	Copper
🐑	Main wool growing area
⋰	Deposit of Fullers Earth

A   B   C   D

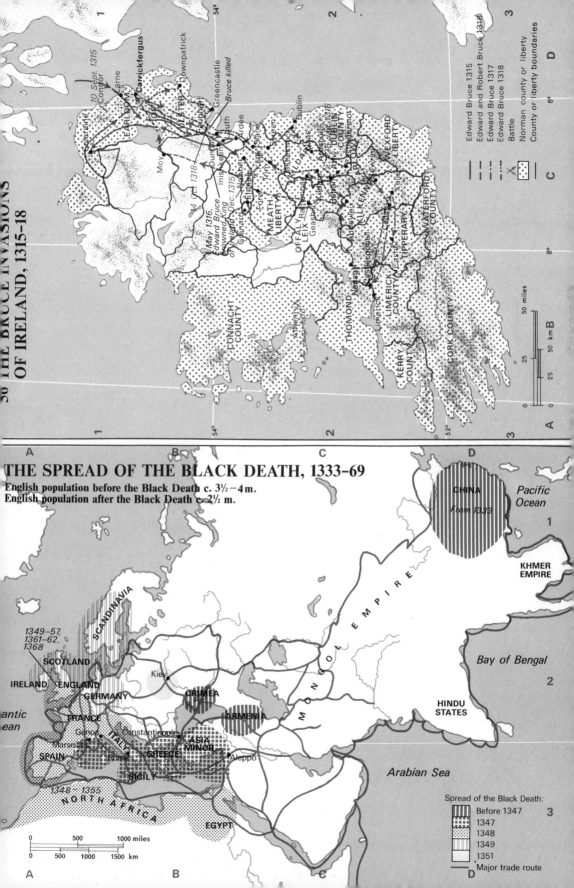

30 THE BRUCE INVASIONS OF IRELAND, 1315-18

Map 1 (top) labels:

10 Sept. 1315
Condror
Carrickfergus
Larne
Downpatrick
Greencastle
Bruce killed
Faughart
Dundalk
Ardee
Ath
Louth
Moy
14 Oct. 1318
May 1316
Edward Bruce crowned King of Ireland Dec. 1315
Granard
Dublin
ULSTER
E. KILDOM
Coleraine
Iniskeen
MEATH LIBERTY
OFFALY LEIX
Geashill
Rathangan
Forest
Elmore
Naas
Kildare
DUBLIN COUNTY
WEXFORD LIBERTY
WATERFORD COUNTY
KILKENNY
TIPPERARY
Abbeyleix
Castledermot
THOMOND
Nenagh
LIMERICK COUNTY
Limerick
KERRY COUNTY
CONNACHT COUNTY
Athenry
Aug. 1316
CORK COUNTY

Edward Bruce 1315
Edward and Robert Bruce 1316
Edward Bruce 1317
Edward Bruce 1318
Battle
Norman county or liberty
County or liberty boundaries

50 miles
km B
50 km
25
25
0

D
C
B
A

THE SPREAD OF THE BLACK DEATH, 1333-69

English population before the Black Death c. 3½ – 4 m.
English population after the Black Death c. 2½ m.

A   B   C   D

CHINA
From 1333

Pacific Ocean

KHMER EMPIRE

MONGOL EMPIRE

Bay of Bengal

1349–57,
1361–62,
1368

SCANDINAVIA

SCOTLAND

IRELAND   ENGLAND

GERMANY

Kiev

CRIMEA

ARMENIA

HINDU STATES

FRANCE

Genoa

ITALY

Constantinople

Marseilles

Rome

SPAIN

GREECE

ASIA MINOR

Aleppo

Arabian Sea

SICILY

1348 – 1355
NORTH AFRICA

EGYPT

antic ean

Atlantic Ocean

0   500   1000 miles
0   500   1000   1500 km

Spread of the Black Death:
Before 1347
1347
1348
1349
1351
Major trade route

A   B   C   D

1

2

3

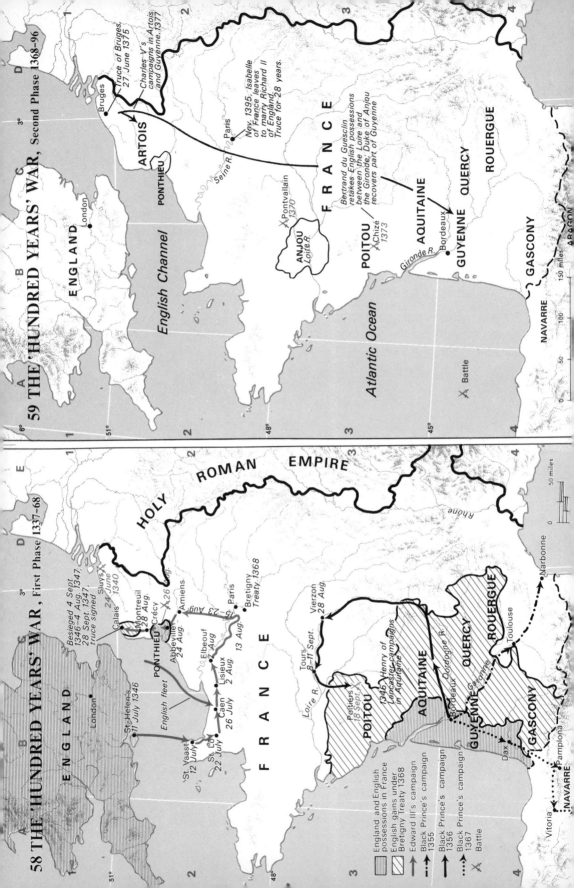

59 THE 'HUNDRED YEARS' WAR', Second Phase 1368–96

58 THE 'HUNDRED YEARS' WAR', First Phase 1337–68

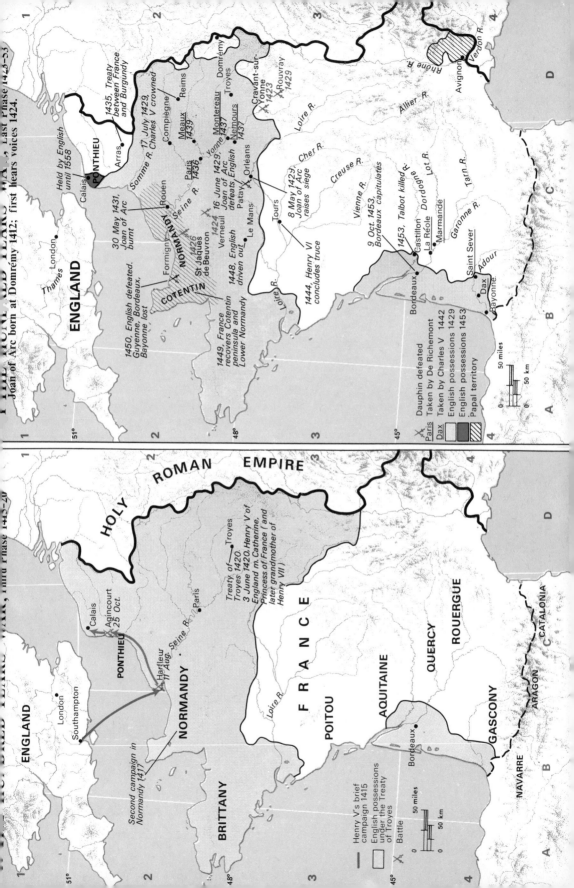

THE HUNDRED YEARS WAR, Last Phase 1428–53
Joan of Arc born at Domrémy 1412; first hears voices 1424.

THE HUNDRED YEARS WAR, Third Phase 1415–20

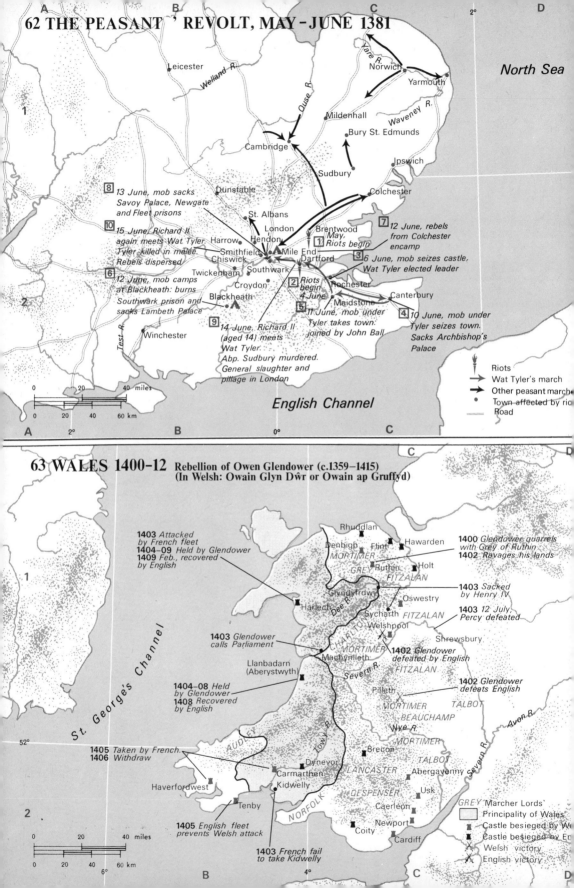

62 THE PEASANT 'S REVOLT, MAY–JUNE 1381

North Sea

Leicester

Welland R.

Ouse R.

Yare R.

Norwich

Yarmouth

Waveney R.

Mildenhall

Cambridge

Bury St. Edmunds

Ipswich

Sudbury

Dunstable

Colchester

8 *13 June, mob sacks
Savoy Palace, Newgate
and Fleet prisons*

St. Albans

Brentwood

7 *12 June, rebels
from Colchester
encamp*

10 *15 June, Richard II
again meets Wat Tyler.
Tyler killed in melée.
Rebels dispersed.*

London

Hendon

1 *May,
Riots begin*

Harrow

Mile End

Smithfield

Chiswick

Southwark

Dartford

3 *6 June, mob seizes castle,
Wat Tyler elected leader*

6 *12 June, mob camps
at Blackheath: burns
Southwark prison and
sacks Lambeth Palace*

Twickenham

Croydon

Blackheath

2 *Riots
begin
4 June*

Rochester

Maidstone

Canterbury

5 *11 June, mob under
Tyler takes town:
joined by John Ball*

4 *10 June, mob under
Tyler seizes town.
Sacks Archbishop's
Palace*

Test R.

Winchester

9 *14 June, Richard II
(aged 14) meets
Wat Tyler.
Abp. Sudbury murdered.
General slaughter and
pillage in London*

English Channel

	Riots
→	Wat Tyler's march
➤	Other peasant march
•	Town affected by riot
---	Road

0   20   40 miles

0   20   40   60 km

2°   0°

63 WALES 1400–12   Rebellion of Owen Glendower (c.1359–1415)
(In Welsh: Owain Glyn Dŵr or Owain ap Gruffyd)

Rhuddlan

*1403 Attacked
by French fleet*
1404-09 Held by Glendower
*1409 Feb., recovered
by English*

Denbigh

Flint

Hawarden

*1400 Glendower quarrels
with Grey of Ruthin*
1402 Ravages his lands

MORTIMER

Holt

GREY   Ruthin

FITZALAN

Glyndyfrdwy

Oswestry

*1403 Sacked
by Henry IV*

Harlech

Dee R.

Sycharth

FITZALAN

Welshpool

*1403 12 July,
Percy defeated*

CHARLTON

Shrewsbury

*1403 Glendower
calls Parliament*

MORTIMER

Machynlleth

*1402 Glendower
defeated by English*

Llanbadarn
(Aberystwyth)

Severn R.

FITZALAN

*1404-08 Held
by Glendower*
*1408 Recovered
by English*

St. George's Channel

Pilleth

*1402 Glendower
defeats English*

MORTIMER   TALBOT

BEAUCHAMP

Wye R.

AUDLEY

Towy R.

MORTIMER

Brecon

1405 Taken by French.
1406 Withdraw

Dynevor

LANCASTER

TALBOT

Abergavenny

Severn R.

Avon R.

Carmarthen

Kidwelly

DESPENSER

Usk

Haverfordwest

NORFOLK

Caerleon

GREY *'Marcher Lords'*

Tenby

Newport

Coity

Cardiff

*1405 English fleet
prevents Welsh attack*

*1403 French fail
to take Kidwelly*

	Principality of Wales
⬛	Castle besieged by Welsh
⬛	Castle besieged by English
✕	Welsh victory
✕	English victory

0   20   40 miles

0   20   40   60 km

52°

6°   4°

Aberdeen

Tay R.

St. Andrews

56°

Glasgow   Leith

Clyde R.

Southern Uplands

Nith R.   *Tweed R.*

Esk R.   Cheviot Hills

Newcastle

Carlisle   *Tyne R.*   Durham

ISLE OF
MAN

Tees R.

Swale R.

Ure R.   *Derwent R.*

Ouse R.   York

54°

Ribble R.   *Wharfe*   *Aire R.*   Hull

Liverpool

Mersey R.

Derwent R.

Beaumaris   *Idle R.*   Lincoln

Conway   Chester   *Trent R.*

Caernarvon   Boston

Dee R.   Nottingham

Irish Sea   Rugeley

Don R.   *Witham R.*

Stourbridge   Lynn   *Yare R.*

Norwich

Severn R.   *Welland R.*   Yarmouth

Ouse R.   *Waveney R.*

Avon R.   Northampton   Cambridge

Tewkesbury   Ipswich

52°

Haverfordwest   Gloucester   East Anglian Heights

Wye R.

Milford
Haven   Tenby   Carmarthen   Woodstock   *Lea R.*

Chepstow   Cotswold Hills   Oxford   Chiltern Hills

Thames R.   London

Bristol   Rochester

Avon R.   *Test R.*   *Wey R.*   Sandwich

Bridgwater   Mendip Hills   *Medway R.*

Exmoor   Winchester   Chiddingfold   Romney

Exe R.   *Parrett R.*   *The Weald*   Shoreham   Winchelsea

Lyme   Southampton   Pevensey

Dartmoor   Regis   *Stour R.*   Poole   Portsmouth

Exeter   Bridport   St. Helen's

Tamar R.   Sidmouth   Melcombe Regis

Teignmouth   Otterton   Weymouth   Wareham

Exmouth

Plymouth   Kingswear

Fowey   Dartmouth

St. Ives

English Channel

North Sea

	Port
	Principal inland town
	University
	Coal
	Glass
	Iron
	Wool
	Hides
	Tin
	Lead
	Cloth

Shambaugh Library

0   25   50 miles

0   25   50 km

A   4°   B   2°   C   0°   D

0°

65 THE WARS OF THE ROSES, 1455–71, 1485

North Sea

Irish Sea

Lancastrian castle
Yorkist castle
Lancastrian victory
Yorkist victory

Norham
Wark
25 Apr. 1464
Hedgeley Moor
Bamburgh
Dunstanburgh
Alnwick
Warkworth
Hexham
8 May 1468
Newcastle
Lumley
Carlisle
Brancepeth
Raby
Appleby
Barnard Castle
Bolton
Middleham
Masham
Skelton
Richmond
Sheriff Hutton
Lancaster
Knaresborough
Spofforth
York
Cawood
Wressell
Ravenspur *1471*
29 March 1461
Towton Moor
30 Dec. 1460
Wakefield
Sandal
Conisborough
Tickhill
Liverpool
Henry VII defeats
Lambert Simnel's rebellion
Bolingbroke
Tattershall
Rhuddlan
Beaumaris
Conway
Denbigh
Ruthin
Chester
Newcastle-under-Lyme
Stokefield
16 June 1487
Newark
Belvoir
Harlech
Tutbury
23 Sept. 1459
Blore Heath
Castle Rising
Caist
Bosworth Field
22 Aug. 1485
Fotheringhay
Wingfield
Stokesay
Ludlow
Ludford Bridge
Warwick
Kenilworth
Northampton
10 July 1460
Framlingham
1468
Edward IV restored 1471–83
2 Feb. 1461
Mortimer's Cross
Tewkesbury
4 May 1471
Edgcott
1469
Pleshey
Grosmont
White Castle
Skenfrith
Haverfordwest
Kidwelly
Abergavenny
Raglan
Gloucester
St. Albans
22 May 1455
St. David's
Milford Haven
Swansea
Usk
Berkeley
Wallingford
17 Feb. 1461
Barnet
14 Apr. 1471
London
Pembroke
Manorbier
Caerphilly
Ogmore
Cardiff
Windsor
Farnham
Reigate
Leeds
Dover
Tiverton
Arundel
Steyning
Herstmonceux
Okehampton
Portchester
Bramber
Pevensey
Compton
Corfe
Carisbrooke

English Channel

0   25   50 miles
0   25   50 km

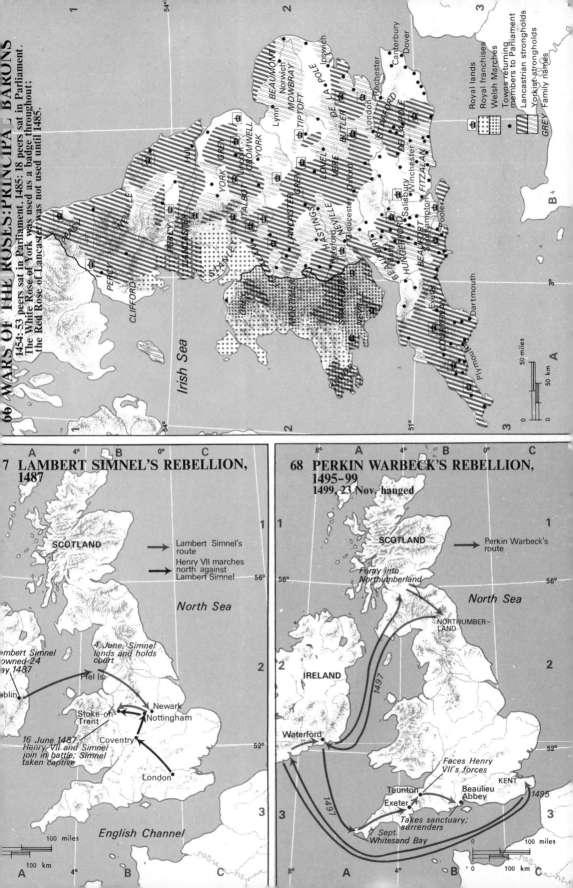

66 WARS OF THE ROSES: PRINCIPAL BARONS

1454: 53 peers sat in Parliament. 1485: 18 peers sat in Parliament.
The White Rose of York was used as a badge throughout;
the Red Rose of Lancaster was not used until 1485.

Royal lands
Royal franchises
Welsh Marches
Towns returning members to Parliament
Lancastrian strongholds
Yorkist strongholds
GREY Family names

PERCY
NEVILLE
CLIFFORD
PERCY
HULL
GREY
LANCASTER
STANLEY
YORK
YORK
TALBOT
GREY
LUDLOW
CROMWELL
YORK
LANCASTER
GREY
HASTINGS
NEVILLE
STAFFORD
HEREFORD
GLOUCESTER
LOVEL
VERE
OXFORD
BEAUMONT
MOWBRAY
TIPTOFT
DE LA POLE
BUTLER
STAFFORD
DE LA POLE
BEAUFORT
HUNGERFORD
BEAUFORT
SALISBURY
WINCHESTER
FITZALAN
COURTENAY

Lynn
Norwich
Ipswich
London
Canterbury
Dover
Rochester
Southampton
Poole
Salisbury
Oxford
Coventry
Exeter
Dartmouth
Plymouth

Irish Sea

50 miles
50 km

A
B
1
2
3
54°
51°
3°

---

67 LAMBERT SIMNEL'S REBELLION, 1487

→ Lambert Simnel's route
➤ Henry VII marches north against Lambert Simnel

SCOTLAND

North Sea

Lambert Simnel crowned 24 May 1487

4 June, Simnel lands and holds court
Piel Is.

Dublin

Newark
Nottingham
Stoke-on-Trent

16 June 1487, Henry VII and Simnel join in battle; Simnel taken captive
Coventry

London

English Channel

100 miles
100 km

A
B
C
1
2
3
4°
0°
56°
52°
4°

---

68 PERKIN WARBECK'S REBELLION, 1495–99

1499, 23 Nov. hanged

→ Perkin Warbeck's route

SCOTLAND

Foray into Northumberland

North Sea

NORTHUMBER–LAND

IRELAND

1497

Waterford

1497

Taunton
Exeter
Beaulieu Abbey

Faces Henry VII's forces

KENT

1495

Takes sanctuary; surrenders
Sept. Whitesand Bay

100 miles
100 km

A
B
C
1
2
3
8°
4°
0°
56°
52°
8°
4°
0°

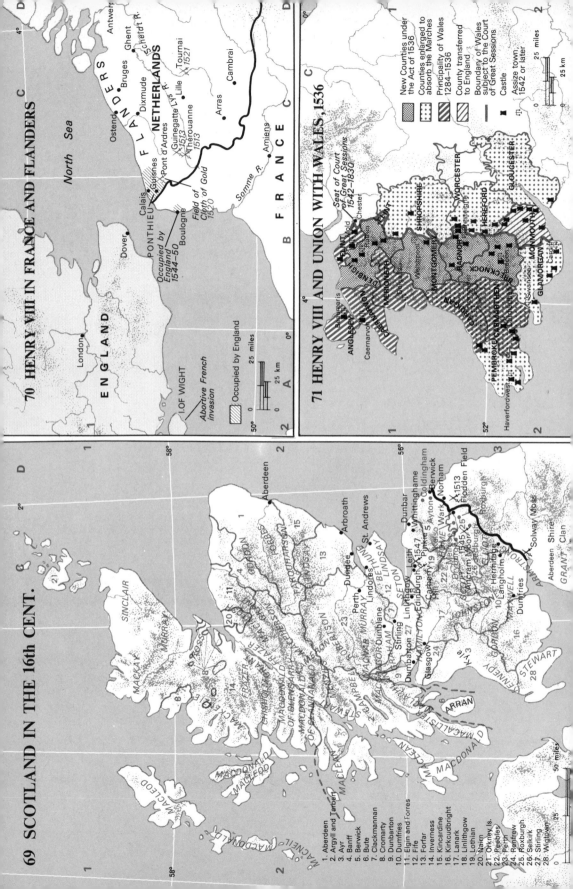

69 SCOTLAND IN THE 16th CENT.

58°

2°

D

1

Aberdeen

Arbroath

St. Andrews

Dundee

LINDSAY

BETHUN

Perth

Lindores

Dunblane

DRUMMOND

Stirling

Dumbarton

Glasgow

Edinburgh

Leith

Linlithgow

Dunbar

Whittinghame

Coldingham

X 1513 Flodden Field

Ayton

Berwick

Norham

Wark

Kelso

Pinkie 5

Carberry Hill

Ancrum

Jedburgh

Roxburgh

Langholm

Hermitage

Dumfries

Solway Moss

Aberdeen Shire

GRANT

Clan

56°

3

MACLEOD

MACNEIL

MACDONALD

MACLEAN

MACALLISTER

MACDONALD OF SLEAT

ARRAN

KYLE

STEWART

CAMPBELL

MACDONALD OF GLENGARRY

GRAHAM

ROBERTSON

FRAZER

CHISHOLM

MURRAY

MACKAY

SINCLAIR

GORDON

FORBES

FARQUHARSON

MACNAB

SETON

HAMILTON

KENNEDY

STEWART

GORDON

JOHNSTON

MAXWELL

ARMSTRONG

1. Aberdeen
2. Argyll and Tarbert
3. Ayr
4. Banff
5. Berwick
6. Bute
7. Clackmannan
8. Cromarty
9. Dunbarton
10. Dumfries
11. Elgin and Forres
12. Fife
13. Forfar
14. Inverness
15. Kincardine
16. Kirkcudbright
17. Lanark
18. Linlithgow
19. Lothian
20. Nairn
21. Orkney Is.
22. Peebles
23. Perth
24. Renfrew
25. Roxburgh
26. Selkirk
27. Stirling
28. Wigtown

0 ___ 25 ___ 50 miles

---

70 HENRY VIII IN FRANCE AND FLANDERS

North Sea

ENGLAND

London

Dover

I. OF WIGHT

Abortive French invasion

Calais

Guisnes

Occupied by England 1544–50

Boulogne

Field of Cloth of Gold 1520

PONTHIEU

Somme R.

Amiens

Arras

Cambrai

FRANCE

Antwerp

Scheldt R.

Ghent

Bruges

Dixmude

Ostend

FLANDERS

Lille

Tournai 1527

Guinegatte 1513

Pont d'Ardres

Therouanne 1513

NETHERLANDS

North Sea

50°

0°

Occupied by England

0 ___ 25 km

0 ___ 25 miles

---

71 HENRY VIII AND UNION WITH WALES, 1536

Chester

Holt

Ruthin

Flint

Mold

Denbigh

FLINT

DENBIGH

Beaumaris

ANGLESEY

Caernarvon

CAERNARVON

MERIONETH

MONTGOMERY

Welshpool

Montgomery

RADNOR

CARDIGAN

BRECKNOCK

Brecon

Cardigan

Haverfordwest

PEMBROKE

CARMARTHEN

Carmarthen

Swansea

GLAMORGAN

Cardiff

MONMOUTH

HEREFORD

Hereford

SHROPSHIRE

Shrewsbury

WORCESTER

Worcester

GLOUCESTER

Gloucester

Seat of Court of Great Sessions 1542–1830

	New Counties under the Act of 1536
	Counties enlarged to absorb the Marches
	Principality of Wales 1284–1536
	County transferred to England
	Boundary of Wales subject to the Court of Great Sessions
✕	Castle
⌘	Assize town, 1542 or later

0 ___ 25 km

0 ___ 25 miles

52°

4°

72 THE REFORMATION

A   9°   B   6°   C   3°   D   0°   E

1

Dornoch

Fortrose   Elgin

Aberdeen

57°

Brechin

*John Knox preaching
from 1559 at Dundee,
Perth and St. Andrews*

Dunkeld

Lismore   Perth   Dundee
Dunblane   St. Andrews

Iona

2

Glasgow

To York

Raphoe   Derry   Whithorn   Carlisle   Durham

Connor

Killala   Clogher   Dromore   Down
Achonry   Armagh   Jervaulx   Fountains   Bridlington

ayo   Kilmore   York   54°
Elphin   Ardagh   Whalley
Tuam   Meath   Pontefract
Annaghdown   Clonmacnois   **CHESTER**   Doncaster
Clonfert   Dublin   Badsley   Louth
ora   Kilmacduagh   Kildare   Lincoln
Killaloe   Kirkstead
Limerick   Ossory   Leighlin   Lenton
ert   Cashel   Ferns
Emly

St. Asaph   Norwich
Bangor   Chester   Lichfield   Peterborough   Ely
Coventry   **PETERBOROUGH**
Lismore   Waterford   Worcester   **OXFORD**   Woburn
Hereford   Oxford   Colchester
Cork   Cloyne   St. David's   Gloucester   London
ss   **GLOUCESTER**   **WESTMINISTER**   Rochester
(for 10 years only)
Llandaff   Bath   Reading   Canterbury

3

BRISTOL   Wells   Salisbury   Winchester   51°
Glastonbury   Chichester

Exeter   *To Bristol*

Dioceses created by Henry VIII

Mainly Lutheran affected area

England: supporting Pilgrimage of Grace
Scotland: mainly loyal to Holy See

Old diocesan boundaries

Cathedral town

Monasteries whose abbots
were executed by Henry VIII

50   100 miles

50   100   150 km

6°   C   3°   D   E

4

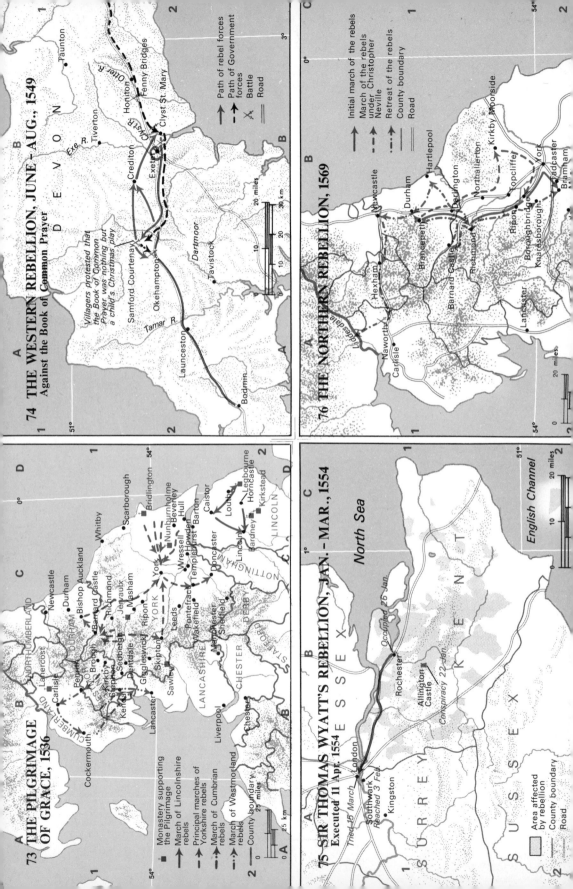

73 THE PILGRIMAGE OF GRACE, 1536

74 THE WESTERN REBELLION, JUNE–AUG., 1549
Against the Book of Common Prayer

75 SIR THOMAS WYATT'S REBELLION, JAN.–MAR., 1554
Executed 11 Apr. 1554

76 THE NORTHERN REBELLION, 1569

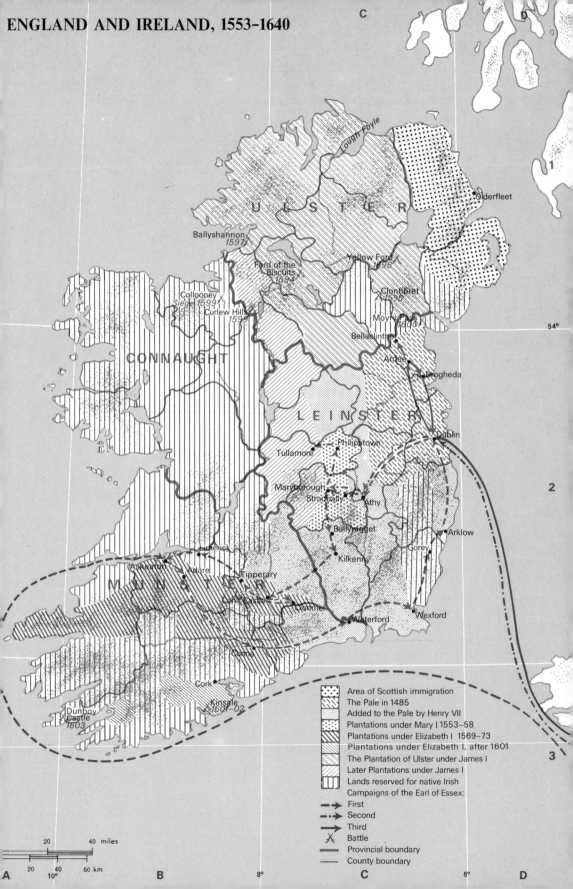

ENGLAND AND IRELAND, 1553–1640

C

D

Lough Foyle

1

Olderfleet

U L S T E R

Ballyshannon
1597

Yellow Ford
1598

Ford of the
Biscuits
1594

Clontibret
1595

Collooney
Siege 1599 X
Curlew Hills
1599

Moyry Pass
1600

54°

Bellaolinthe

C O N N A U G H T

Ardee

Drogheda

L E I N S T E R

Dublin

Philipstown

Tullamore

Maryborough

Stradbally

Athy

2

Ballynaget

Arklow

Kilkenny

Gorey

Limerick

Askeaton

Adare

Tipperary

M U N S T E R

Cahir Castle

Clonmel

Wexford

Waterford

Conna

Cork

Kinsale
1601–02

Dunboy
Castle
1603

3

	Area of Scottish immigration
	The Pale in 1485
	Added to the Pale by Henry VII
	Plantations under Mary I 1553–58
	Plantations under Elizabeth I 1569–73
	Plantations under Elizabeth I, after 1601
	The Plantation of Ulster under James I
	Later Plantations under James I
	Lands reserved for native Irish

Campaigns of the Earl of Essex:

➡ - ➡	First
➡ - ➡	Second
➡	Third
X	Battle
	Provincial boundary
	County boundary

20   40 miles

20   40
      60 km

A   B   8°   C   6°   D

10°

78 ECONOMIC AND SOCIAL LIFE UNDER THE TUDORS

Population: 1570 – 4.1 m.
          1600 – 4.8 m.

Thames R. Navigable river
        Lead
        Tin
        Coal
        Iron
        Toolmakers
        Loriners
        Mailers
        Nails
        Salt
        Cloth
        Wool
        Cotton
        Armaments
        Glass
        Dockyards
        Alum
        University
        Chief port
        Road

North Sea

Irish Sea

Sea route bringing coal from Newcastle to London

St. Andrews
Leith
Glasgow
Newcastle
Tyne R.
Whitby
Kendal
Malton
Derwent R.
Blackburn
Hull
Bury
Rochdale
WEST RIDING
Humber
Liverpool
Beaumaris
Conway
Chester
Derwent R.
Idle R.
Trent R.
Witham R.
Caernarvon
Nantwich
DERBY-SHIRE
Newark
Boston
Oswestry
Stafford
Nottingham
Welland R.
Shrewsbury
Severn R.
Lynn
Ouse R.
Yare R.
Kidderminster
Birmingham
Norwich
Yarmouth
Clee Hills
Droitwich
Worcester
Cambridge
Hereford
Tewkesbury
Ipswich
Forest of Dean
Gloucester
Oxford
Severn Basin
Haverfordwest
Lea
Chepstow
Milford Haven
London
Tenby
Bristol
Deptford
Rochester
Woolwich
Chatham
Sandwich
Mendips
Medway R.
Canterbury
WILTSHIRE
The Weald
Bridgwater
SOMERSET
HAMPSHIRE
Romney
DEVON
Lyme Regis
Southampton
Shoreham
Winchelsea
Sidmouth
Exe R.
Parrett R.
Bridport
Poole
Portsmouth
Pevensey
Exeter
Otterton
Wareham
St. Helen's
Teignmouth
Exmouth
Weymouth
Melcombe Regis
Plymouth
Kingswear
St. Ives
CORNWALL
Fowey
Dartmouth

English Channel

0   25   50 miles
0   25   50 km

1580–1640: Portugal under the Spanish Crown

Pacific Ocean

JAPAN

CHINA

TARTARY

MUSCOVY
COMPANY
1554

RUSSIA

EASTLAND
COMPANY 1579

LEVANT COMPANY 1592

PERSIA

INDIA

EAST INDIA
COMPANY
1600

Indian Ocean

AUSTRALIA
(unknown)

MERCHANT
ADVENTURERS
1407

ENGLAND

PORTUGAL

SPAIN

MOROCCO
COMPANY 1596

BARBARY

EGYPT

A F R I C A

GUINEA COMPANY
1588

Atlantic Ocean

HUDSON'S BAY
COMPANY 1670

PLYMOUTH
COMPANY
1696

LONDON
COMPANY 1606

NEW SPAIN

PANAMA

Roanoke

1st
2nd
4th
3rd

PERU

CHILE

BRAZIL

Pacific Ocean

PLYMOUTH   English trading company
           England and English
           possessions
           Portugal and Portuguese
           settlements
           Spain and Spanish
           settlements
           Line of division between
           Portugal and Spain by
           Treaty of Tordesillas
           7 June 1494
           (Long. 48°–49°w.)

Principal Voyages 1488–1585:
Chancellor   1533–5
Frobisher   1576
Drake   1570
Grenville   1585
Dias   1488
Colombus   1492
Gama   1498–9
Cabot   1497

0   1500   3000 miles
0   1500   3000 km

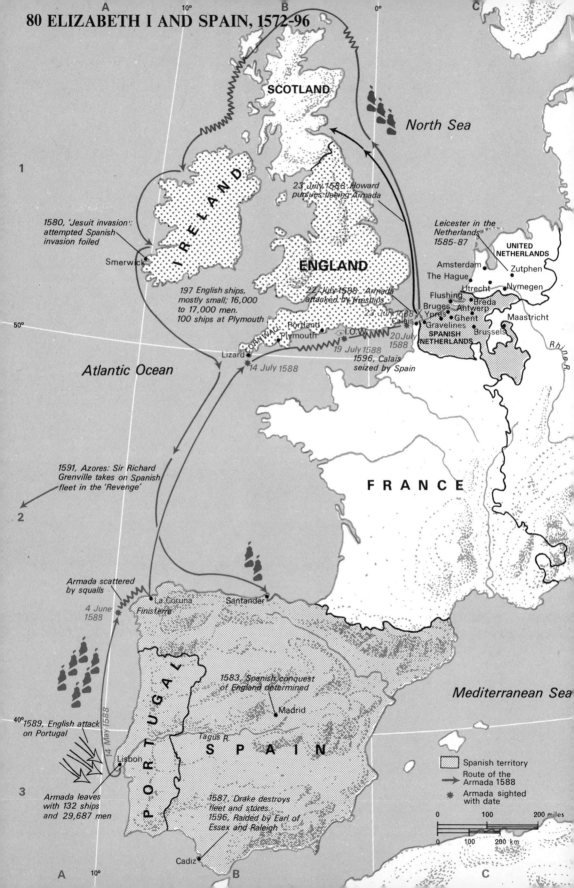

80 ELIZABETH I AND SPAIN, 1572-96

SCOTLAND

North Sea

23 July 1588: Howard pursues fleeing Armada

1580, 'Jesuit invasion': attempted Spanish invasion foiled

Smerwick

IRELAND

ENGLAND

Leicester in the Netherlands 1585-87

UNITED NETHERLANDS

Amsterdam
The Hague
Utrecht
Zutphen
Nymegen
Flushing
Breda
Bruges
Antwerp
Ypres
Ghent
Maastricht
Gravelines
Brussels

SPANISH NETHERLANDS

197 English ships, mostly small; 16,000 to 17,000 men. 100 ships at Plymouth

22 July 1588: Armada attacked by fireships

CORNWALL

Portland
Plymouth
I.O.W.
Calais

23 July 1588
20 July 1588
19 July 1588

1596, Calais seized by Spain

50°

Lizard

14 July 1588

Atlantic Ocean

Rhine R.

FRANCE

1591, Azores: Sir Richard Grenville takes on Spanish fleet in the 'Revenge'

2

Armada scattered by squalls

4 June 1588

La Coruña
Finisterre

Santander

1583, Spanish conquest of England determined

Madrid

Mediterranean Sea

40°
1589, English attack on Portugal

14 May 1588

Tagus R.

S P A I N

Lisbon

PORTUGAL

3

Armada leaves with 132 ships and 29,687 men

1587, Drake destroys fleet and stores.
1596, Raided by Earl of Essex and Raleigh

Cadiz

Spanish territory
Route of the Armada 1588
Armada sighted with date

0   100   200 miles
0   100   200 km

A   10°   B   C

THE CIVIL WAR, 1642-53

SCOTLAND

Area controlled by Parliament at 1 May 1643

Area controlled by Parliament at 1 Nov. 1644

✗ Battle

Philiphaugh
1645 ✗

NORTHUMBERLAND

Newburn
1640 ✗ • Newcastle

Durham •

Marston Moor
1644 ✗ • York

Preston
✗ *1648* Adwalton Moor
✗ *1643* Hull ✗

Gainsborough
✗

Rowton Heath
1645 ✗ Winceby ✗

Nantwich
✗ *1644* *1646 May. Charles surrenders to Scots*
Newark
• Nottingham

Lichfield •

Naseby
✗ *1645* Huntingdon
• Newmarket •

Holmby House •
Edge Hill
1642 ✗ Cropredy
✗ *1644*

Worcester ✗

• Oxford

EASTERN ASSOCIATION to raise Parliamentary Army 1643

Lansdown Hill
1643 ✗ Uxbridge ✗
Windsor • London
Donnington ✗ Turnham Green
Castle Hampton Court
Roundway Down ✗ Newbury
1643 ✗ *1644* Basing House
✗ *1645*

Langport
✗ *1645*

Bideford
✗
Stratton ✗

Hurst Castle ✗ Carisbrooke Castle •
IS. OF WIGHT

Lostwithiel
1644 ✗ Bradock Down
✗
Plymouth • Dartmouth
✗

d for the King John Grenville 1653

LY ISLES

0   25   50 miles

0   25   50 km

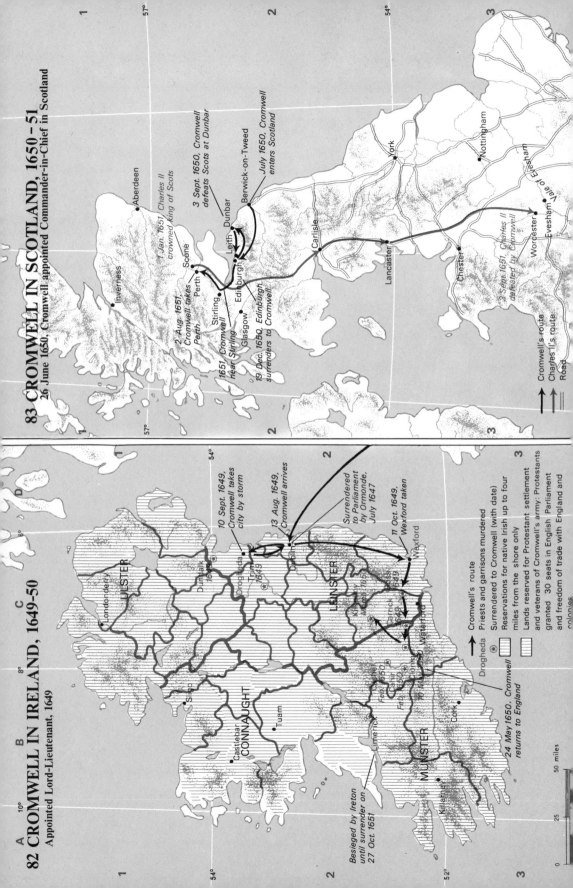

83 CROMWELL IN SCOTLAND, 1650–51
26 June 1650, Cromwell appointed Commander-in-Chief in Scotland

57°

2

54°

3

Aberdeen

Inverness

1 Jan. 1651, Charles II crowned king of Scots

3 Sept. 1650, Cromwell defeats Scots at Dunbar

Dunbar

Berwick-on-Tweed

July 1650, Cromwell enters Scotland

2 Aug. 1651, Cromwell takes Perth

Scone

Perth

Leith

Stirling

Edinburgh

1651 Cromwell near Stirling

Glasgow

19 Dec. 1650, Edinburgh surrenders to Cromwell

Carlisle

York

Nottingham

Lancaster

Chester

Worcester

Evesham

Vale of Evesham

3 Sept. 1651, Charles II defeated by Cromwell

Cromwell's route

Charles II's route

Road

82 CROMWELL IN IRELAND, 1649–50
Appointed Lord-Lieutenant, 1649

A   B   C   D

10°   8°   6°

54°

1

2

ULSTER

Londonderry

Sligo

CONNAUGHT

Castlebar

Tuam

Limerick

MUNSTER

Killarney

Cork

Dundalk

Drogheda

Trim 1649

10 Sept. 1649, Cromwell takes city by storm

13 Aug. 1649, Cromwell arrives

Dublin

LEINSTER

Surrendered to Parliament by Ormonde, July 1647

11 Oct. 1649, Wexford taken

Wexford 1649

Carrick

Waterford

Feb. 1650

Drogheda

Besieged by Ireton until surrender on 27 Oct. 1651

24 May 1650, Cromwell returns to England

Cromwell's route

Priests and garrisons murdered

Surrendered to Cromwell (with date)

Reservations for native Irish up to four miles from the shore only

Lands reserved for Protestant settlement and veterans of Cromwell's army: Protestants granted 30 seats in English Parliament and freedom of trade with England and colonies

0   25   50 miles

52°

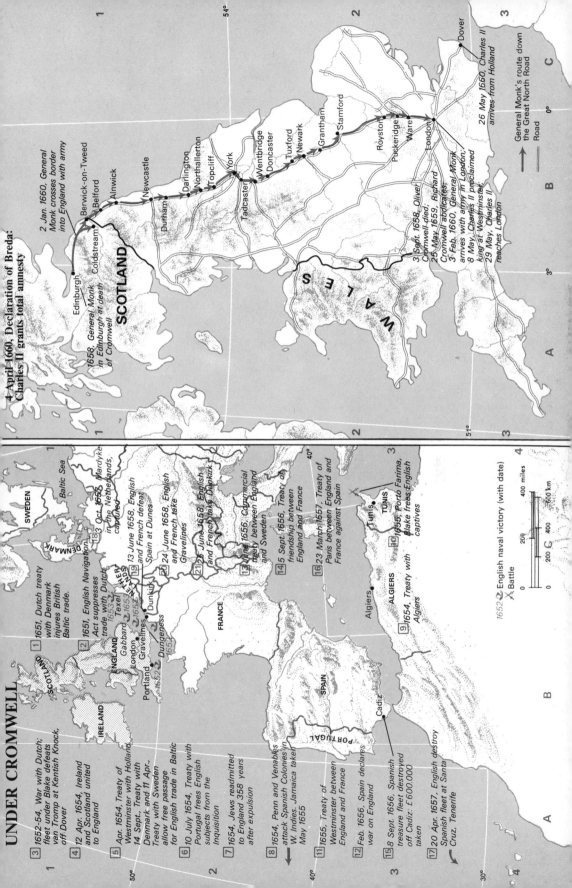

UNDER CROMWELL

4 April 1660, Declaration of Breda: Charles II grants total amnesty

SCOTLAND

WALES

IRELAND

SWEDEN

DENMARK

NETHERLANDS

ENGLAND

FRANCE

SPAIN

PORTUGAL

ALGIERS

TUNIS

Baltic Sea

3 1652–54, War with Dutch: fleet under Blake defeats van Tromp at Kentish Knock, off Dover

4 12 Apr. 1654, Ireland and Scotland united to England

5 Apr. 1654, Treaty of Westminster with Holland, 14 Sept., Treaty with Denmark and 11 Apr., Treaty with Sweden allow free passage for English trade in Baltic

6 10 July 1654, Treaty with Portugal frees English subjects from the Inquisition

7 1654, Jews readmitted to England 358 years after expulsion

8 1654, Penn and Venables attack Spanish Colonies in W. Indies. Jamaica taken May 1655

9 1654, Treaty with Algiers

10 1655, Porto Farina, Blake frees English captives

11 1655, Treaty of Westminster between England and France

12 Feb. 1656, Spain declares war on England

13 June 1656, Commercial treaty between England and Sweden

14 5 Sept. 1656, Treaty of friendship between England and France

15 8 Sept. 1656, Spanish treasure fleet destroyed off Cadiz: £600,000 taken

16 23 March 1657, Treaty of Paris between England and France against Spain

17 20 Apr. 1657, English destroy Spanish fleet at Santa Cruz, Tenerife

18 3 Oct. 1652, Mardyke in the Netherlands, captured

19 1651, English Navigation Act suppresses trade with Dutch

20 24 June 1658, English and French take Gravelines

21 25 June 1658, English and French take Dunkirk

22 13 June 1658, English and French defeat Spain at Dunes

1 1651, Dutch treaty with Denmark injures British Baltic trade

2 1651, English Navigation Act suppresses trade with Dutch

1652 English naval victory (with date)
✗ Battle

General Monk's route down the Great North Road

2 Jan. 1660, General Monk crosses border into England with army

1658, General Monk in Edinburgh at death of Cromwell

3 Sept. 1658, Oliver Cromwell died.
25 May 1659, Richard Cromwell abdicates.
3 Feb. 1660, General Monk arrives with army in London;
8 May, Charles II proclaimed king at Westminster.
29 May, Charles II reaches London

26 May 1660, Charles II arrives from Holland

Edinburgh · Coldstream · Berwick-on-Tweed · Belford · Alnwick · Newcastle · Durham · Darlington · Northallerton · Topcliff · York · Tadcaster · Wentbridge · Doncaster · Tuxford · Newark · Grantham · Stamford · Royston · Puckeridge · Ware · London · Dover

Portland · Gabbard · Texel · Dungeness · Dunkirk · Gravelines · Cadiz · Algiers · Tunis

0 200 400 miles
0 200 400 600 km

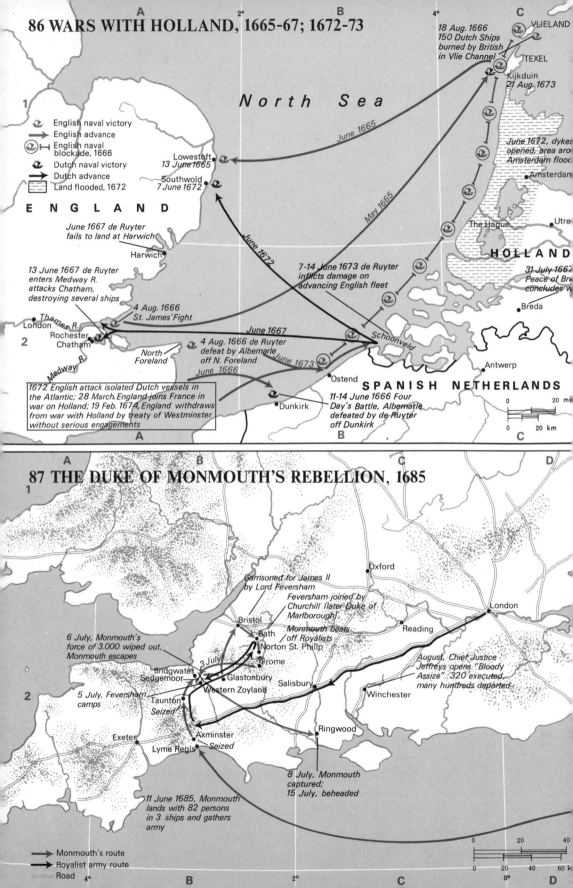

86 WARS WITH HOLLAND, 1665-67; 1672-73

North Sea

18 Aug. 1666
150 Dutch Ships
burned by British
in Vlie Channel

VLIELAND

TEXEL

Kijkduin
21 Aug. 1673

June 1665

May 1665

June 1672, dykes
opened, area around
Amsterdam flooded

Amsterdam

Lowestoft
13 June 1665

Southwold
7 June 1672

E N G L A N D

The Hague

H O L L A N D

Utre[cht]

June 1667 de Ruyter
fails to land at Harwich

31 July 1667
Peace of Bre[da]
concludes w[...]

Harwich

Breda

13 June 1667 de Ruyter
enters Medway R.
attacks Chatham,
destroying several ships

7-14 June 1673 de Ruyter
inflicts damage on
advancing English fleet

Thames R.
London
Rochester
Chatham

4 Aug. 1666
St. James' Fight

Medway R.

North
Foreland

4 Aug. 1666 de Ruyter
defeat by Albemarle
off N. Foreland

June 1667

Schoonveld

Antwerp

June 1673

June 1666

1672 English attack isolated Dutch vessels in
the Atlantic; 28 March, England joins France in
war on Holland; 19 Feb. 1674, England withdraws
from war with Holland by treaty of Westminster
without serious engagements

Ostend

Dunkirk

11-14 June 1666 Four
Day's Battle, Albemarle
defeated by de Ruyter
off Dunkirk

S P A N I S H   N E T H E R L A N D S

0   20 mi[les]

0   20 km

Legend:
- English naval victory
- English advance
- English naval blockade, 1666
- Dutch naval victory
- Dutch advance
- Land flooded, 1672

87 THE DUKE OF MONMOUTH'S REBELLION, 1685

Oxford

Garrisoned for James II
by Lord Feversham

Feversham joined by
Churchill (later Duke of
Marlborough)

Monmouth beats
off Royalists

London

Bristol

Bath

Norton St. Philip

Reading

6 July, Monmouth's
force of 3,000 wiped out,
Monmouth escapes

3 July

Frome

August, Chief Justice
Jeffreys opens "Bloody
Assize"; 320 executed,
many hundreds deported

Bridgwater
Sedgemoor

Glastonbury

Salisbury

5 July, Feversham
camps

Western Zoyland

Winchester

Taunton
Seized

Axminster
Seized

Ringwood

Exeter

Lyme Regis

8 July, Monmouth
captured;
15 July, beheaded

11 June 1685, Monmouth
lands with 82 persons
in 3 ships and gathers
army

Legend:
- Monmouth's route
- Royalist army route
- Road

0   20   40

0   20   40   60 [km]

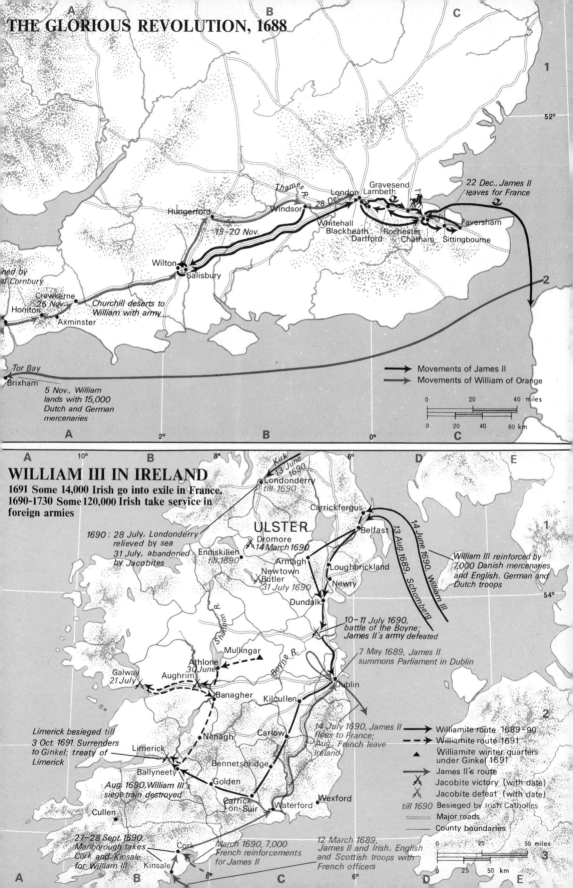

THE GLORIOUS REVOLUTION, 1688

A   B   C

1

52°

Thames R.

Hungerford

Windsor

London
Gravesend
Lambeth

28 Dec.

22 Dec., James II
leaves for France

19–20 Nov.

Whitehall
Blackheath
Dartford

Rochester
Chatham

Faversham

Sittingbourne

Wilton

Salisbury

2

...ned by
d'Cornbury

Crewkerne
25 Nov.

Honiton

Axminster

Churchill deserts to
William with army

Movements of James II
Movements of William of Orange

Tor Bay

Brixham

5 Nov., William
lands with 15,000
Dutch and German
mercenaries

0   20   40 miles

0   20 40 60 km

A   2°   B   0°   C

A 10°   B   8°   D   E

WILLIAM III IN IRELAND

**1691 Some 14,000 Irish go into exile in France,
1690-1730 Some 120,000 Irish take service in
foreign armies**

Kirk
13 June
1690

Londonderry
till 1690

Carrickfergus

1

ULSTER

Belfast

1690 : 28 July, Londonderry
relieved by sea
31 July, abandoned
by Jacobites

Enniskillen
till 1690

Dromore
14 March 1690

Armagh

Loughbrickland

14 June 1690, William III

13 Aug 1689, Schomberg

William III reinforced by
7,000 Danish mercenaries
and English, German and
Dutch troops

Newtown
Butler
31 July 1690

Newry

Dundalk

54°

Shannon R.

10–11 July 1690,
battle of the Boyne;
James II's army defeated

Mullingar

Boyne R.

7 May 1689, James II
summons Parliament in Dublin

Athlone
30 June

Galway
21 July

Aughrim

Banagher

Kilcullen

Dublin

2

Limerick besieged till
3 Oct. 1691. Surrenders
to Ginkel; treaty of
Limerick

Nenagh

Carlow

14 July 1690, James II
flees to France;
Aug. French leave
Ireland

Williamite route 1689–90
Williamite route 1691
Williamite winter quarters
under Ginkel 1691
James II's route
Jacobite victory (with date)
Jacobite defeat (with date)
Besieged by Irish Catholics
Major roads
County boundaries

Limerick

Bennetsbridge

Ballyneety

Golden

Aug. 1690, William III's
siege train destroyed

Carrick-
on-Suir

Waterford

Wexford

Cullen

27–28 Sept. 1690,
Marlborough takes
Cork and Kinsale
for William III

Cork

Kinsale

March 1690, 7,000
French reinforcements
for James II

12 March 1689,
James II and Irish, English
and Scottish troops with
French officers

till 1690

0   25   50 miles

0   25   50 km

A   B   8°   C   6°   D   E

3

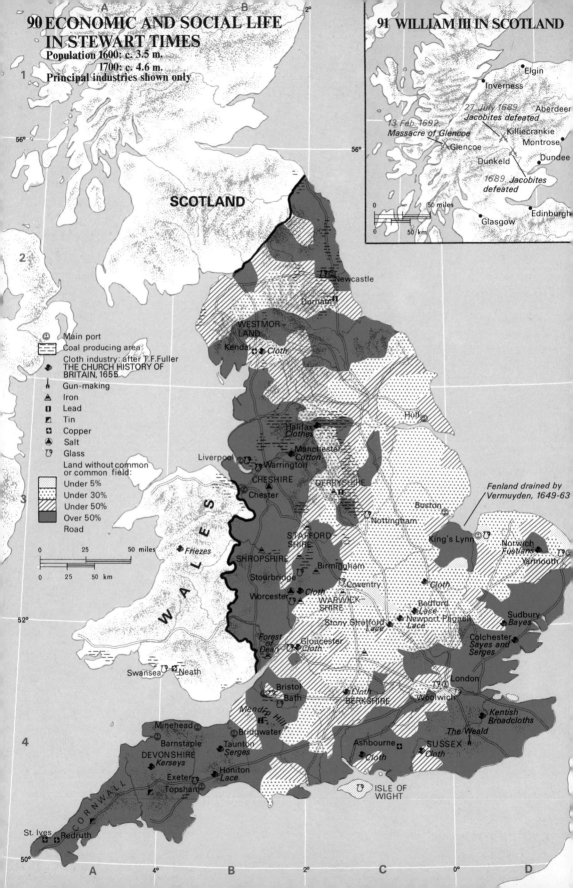

90 ECONOMIC AND SOCIAL LIFE IN STEWART TIMES

Population 1600: c. 3.5 m.
1700: c. 4.6 m.
Principal industries shown only

91 WILLIAM III IN SCOTLAND

Elgin
Inverness
Aberdeen
27 July 1689
Jacobites defeated
13 Feb. 1692
Massacre of Glencoe
Killiecrankie
Montrose
Glencoe
Dundee
Dunkeld
1689 Jacobites
defeated
0   50 miles
0   50 km
Glasgow
Edinburgh

SCOTLAND

Legend

⚓ Main port
Coal producing area
Cloth industry: after T.F.Fuller
THE CHURCH HISTORY OF
BRITAIN, 1655
🔫 Gun-making
△ Iron
▯ Lead
▱ Tin
⊞ Copper
⬥ Salt
♆ Glass

Land without common
or common field:
Under 5%
Under 30%
Under 50%
Over 50%
Road

0   25   50 miles
0   25   50 km

Newcastle
Durham
WESTMOR-
LAND
Kendal ⊞ Cloth
Hull
Halifax
Clothes
Manchester
Cotton
Liverpool
Warrington
CHESHIRE
Chester
DERBYSHIRE
Boston
Nottingham
King's Lynn
Norwich
Fustians
Yarmouth

Fenland drained by
Vermuyden, 1649-63

W A L E S
Friezes
STAFFORD-
SHIRE
SHROPSHIRE
Stourbridge
Worcester Cloth
Birmingham
Coventry
WARWICK-
SHIRE
Stony Stretford
Lace
Cloth
Bedford
Lace
Newport Pagnell
Lace
Sudbury
Bayes
Colchester
Sayes and
Serges

Swansea Neath
Forest
of
Dean
Gloucester
Cloth
Bristol
Bath
BERKSHIRE
Cloth
London
Woolwich
Kentish
Broadcloths
The Weald

Mendip Hills
Minehead
Barnstaple
DEVONSHIRE
Kerseys
Bridgwater
Taunton
Serges
Ashbourne
Cloth
SUSSEX
Cloth

Exeter
Honiton
Lace
Topsham
ISLE OF
WIGHT

CORNWALL
St. Ives Redruth

WAR OF THE LEAGUE OF AUGSBURG, 1689-1697
(Or the Grand Alliance)

SWEDEN

DENMARK

0°

20°

1

Kinsale

ENGLAND

Fleurus:
X 1 July 1690,
League defeated

Neerwinden
3 Aug. 1693,
William III
defeated

BRANDENBURG

Steenkirk
X 3 Aug. 1692

HOLLAND

SAXONY

Beachy Head
10 July 1690
indecisive

Furnes

Ghent

Namur
X 5 June 1692
taken
1 Sept. 1695 taken
by William III

28 Dec. 1692–7 Jan. 1693
besieged: taken by French

Mons

La Hogue
29 May 1692

Charleroi

X 8 Apr. 1691
surrenders

Luxemburg

HOLY

Brest

St. Malo

Versailles

Paris

X 19-21 Oct. 1695
French repulsed

PALATINATE

Mainz
8 Sept. 1689 surrenders

ROMAN

Atlantic Ocean

FRANCE

EMPIRE

2

SAVOY

VENICE

Staffarda
18 Aug. 1690 X

Allies as of 9 July 1686
Allies as of 12 May 1689
X French victory with date
X Alliance victory with date

Marsaglia
4 Oct. 1693

0   100   200   miles

0   100   200 km

PIEDMONT

S P A I N

CATALONIA

Torroella
27 May 1694

A

B

10°

C

D

10°

WAR OF THE SPANISH
SUCCESSION, 1702-13

B

Utrecht

Oudenaarde
11 July 1708

HOLLAND

Venlo
1702

POLAND

London

Bruges
1708

Ghent
1708

Kaiserworth
1702

SAXONY

D

1

Dunkirk

Lille
1708

Brussels

Bonn
1703

Coblenz

Frankfurt

THE EMPIRE

Tournai
1709

SP. NETH.

Landau

Donauwörth

BAVARIA

Malplaquet
11 Sept.
1709

Ramillies
23 May 1706

Ratisbon

Paris

Mons
20 Oct. 1709

Brabant

Ulm

Blenheim
13 Aug. 1704

Danube R.

Vienna

Villingen

AUSTRIA

Marlborough's route
to Blenheim
Prince Eugene's route
Route of French and
Bavarians under Tallard
Fortress held by Allies
Fortress held by French
Allied victory
French victory
England and her allies
France and her allies
Taken by British

FRANCE

SWITZERLAND

SAVOY

Cassano

VENICE

Legnago

2

HUNGARY

Turino

Cretnona

Luzzara

Parma

Carpi

Ghent
1708

Vigo

ct. 1702

PORTUGAL

Saragossa
20 Aug. 1710

Salamanca
1706

Villa Viciosa
X 10 Dec. 1710
Brihuega
9 Dec. 1710

ARAGON

CATALONIA

Barcelona
1705

SARDINIA
Aug. 1708

40°

Ciudad
Rodrigo
1706

Madrid

Almenara
27 July 1710

Talavera

MINORCA
Sept. 1708

Alcantara
1706

Almanza
25 Apr. 1707

Valencia

3

Lisbon

S P A I N

Denia

Alicante
1709

0   100   200   miles

Cadiz

Gibraltar

0°

0   100   200 km

C

D

94 BRITISH POSSESSIONS AFTER THE PEACE OF UTRECHT, 1713
Europe and America

Hudson Bay

HUDSON'S BAY COMPANY

NEWFOUNDLAND

NOVA SCOTIA

MAINE
NEW HAMPSHIRE
MASSACHUSETTS
RHODE ISLAND
CONNECTICUT
NEW YORK
NEW JERSEY
PENNSYLVANIA
DELAWARE
MARYLAND
VIRGINIA
NORTH CAROLINA
SOUTH CAROLINA

WEST INDIES

France grants Britain
right to load produce

Atlantic Ocean

1707, Union between
England and Scotland:
GREAT BRITAIN

SCOTLAND
IRELAND
ENGLAND

HOLY
ROMAN
EMPIRE
AUSTRIA
HUNGARY
FRANCE
SAVOY
SARDINIA
SICILY

MINORCA
1708

S P A I N

Gibraltar

Gulf of Benin

Britain granted right
to transport 4,800 slaves
annually to Spanish America

British possessions
Spanish possessions
French possessions
Austrian possessions
House of Savoy

0   500   1000 miles

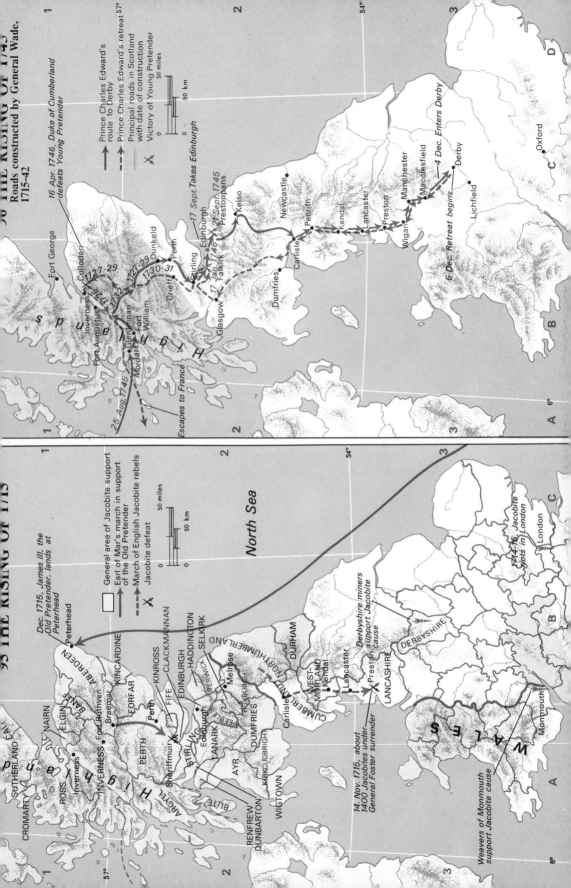

56 THE RISING OF 1745

Roads constructed by General Wade, 1715–42

55 THE RISING OF 1715

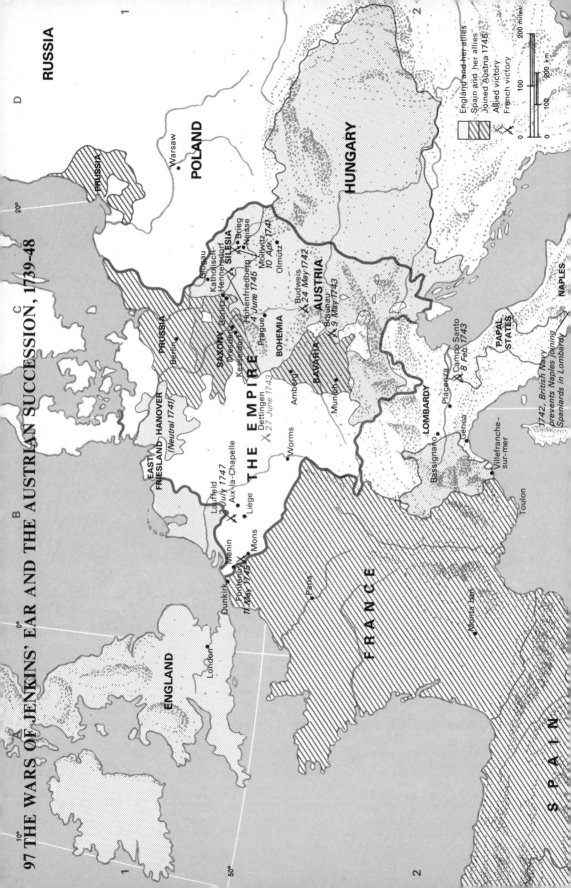

97 THE WARS OF JENKINS' EAR AND THE AUSTRIAN SUCCESSION, 1739-48

RUSSIA

POLAND

Warsaw

PRUSSIA

PRUSSIA

Berlin

Glogau

Katholisch-
Hennersdorf
Görlitz
SILESIA
Brieg
Neisse
Mollwitz,
10 Apr. 1741

HANOVER
(Neutral 1741)

EAST
FRIESLAND

SAXONY
Dresden
Kesselsdorf

Hohenfriedberg,
4 June 1745

Olmütz

Budweis
24 May 1742

AUSTRIA

HUNGARY

BOHEMIA
Prague

THE EMPIRE

Amberg

Braunau
9 May 1743

Dettingen
27 June 1743

Worms

Munich

BAVARIA

London

ENGLAND

Dunkirk
Menin
Fontenoy
11 May 1745
Mons

Laffeld
2 July 1747
Aix-la-Chapelle
Liège

Paris

FRANCE

Montauban

Toulon

SPAIN

LOMBARDY
Placenza
Bassignano
Genoa
Villefranche-
sur-mer

Campo Santo
8 Feb. 1743

PAPAL
STATES

NAPLES

1742, British Navy
prevents Naples joining
Spaniards in Lombardy

England and her allies
Spain and her allies
Joined Austria 1745
Allied victory
French victory

0   100   200 km
0   100   200 miles

98 THE SEVEN YEARS' WAR, 1756–63
(See also maps 99 and 100)

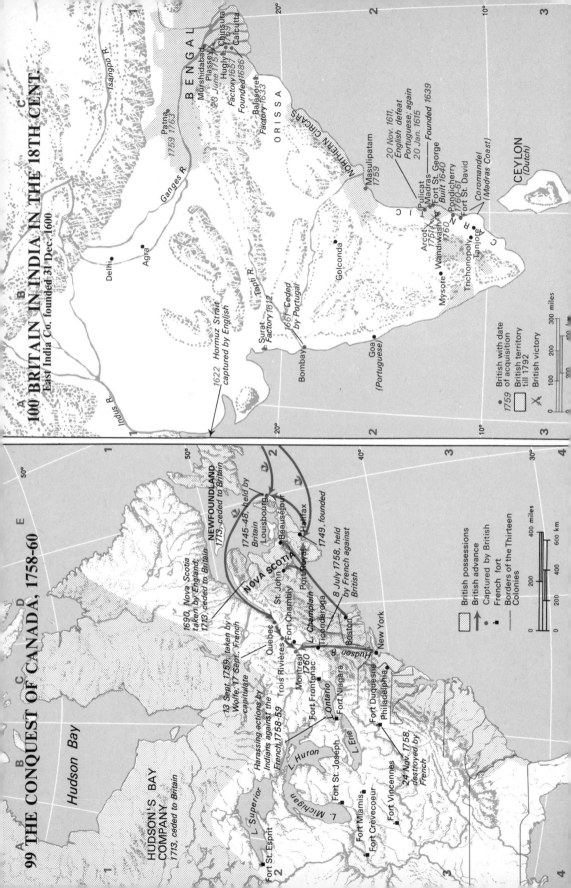

100 BRITAIN IN INDIA IN THE 18TH CENT.

East India Co. founded 31 Dec. 1600

Indus R.

Isangpo R.

Delhi

Agra

Ganges R.

Patna
1759 1763

BENGAL

Murshidabad

Plassey
23 June 1757

Hugly
Factory 1657

Chinsura

Calcutta
Founded 1686

Balasore
Factory 1633

ORISSA

Tapti R.

NORTHERN CIRCARS

Surat
Factory 1612

1661 Ceded
by Portugal

Golconda

Masulipatam
1759

Bombay

Goa
(Portuguese)

Mysore

Arcot
1751

Wandiwash
1760

Trichonopoly

Tanjore

20 Nov. 1611,
English defeat
Portuguese: again
20 Jan. 1615

Pulicat
Madras
Fort St. George
Built 1640
Pondicherry
1760-61
Fort St. David

Founded 1639

Coromandel
(Madras Coast)

CEYLON
(Dutch)

1622 Hormuz Strait
captured by English

● 1759 British with date
of acquisition

British territory
till 1792

✗ British victory

0   100   200   300 miles
0   200   400   600 km

---

99 THE CONQUEST OF CANADA, 1758-60

Hudson Bay

HUDSON'S BAY
COMPANY,
1713, ceded to Britain

Fort St. Esprit

L. Superior

L. Michigan

L. Huron

Fort St. Joseph

Fort Miamis

Fort Crèvecoeur

Fort Vincennes

24 Nov. 1758,
destroyed by
French

Fort Duquesne

Philadelphia

L. Erie

Fort Niagara

L. Ontario

Fort Frontenac

New York

Boston

Hudson

Ticonderoga

L. Champlain

Fort Chambly

Montreal
1760

Trois Rivières

Quebec

13 Sept. 1759, taken by
Wolfe. 17 Sept. French
capitulate

Harassing actions by
Indians against the
French,1758-59

8 July 1758, held
by French against
British

St. John

Port Royal

NOVA SCOTIA

1690, Nova Scotia
taken by England,
1713, ceded to Britain

Halifax
1749, founded

Beausejour

Louisbourg

1745-48, held by
Britain

NEWFOUNDLAND
1713 ceded to Britain

British possessions
British advance
Captured by British
French fort
Borders of the Thirteen
Colonies

0   200   400 miles
0   200   400   600 km

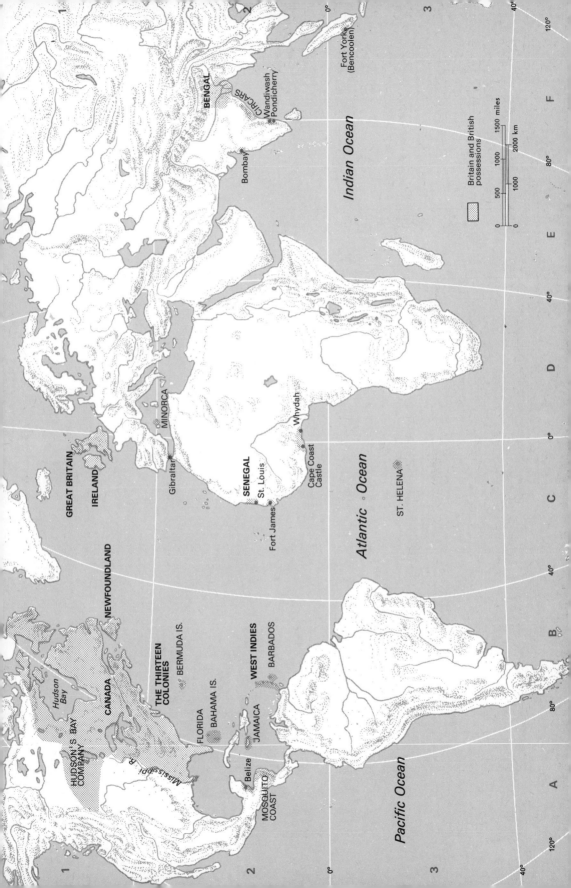

Pacific Ocean

Atlantic Ocean

Indian Ocean

GREAT BRITAIN

IRELAND

NEWFOUNDLAND

CANADA

Hudson Bay

HUDSON'S BAY COMPANY

THE THIRTEEN COLONIES

BERMUDA IS.

FLORIDA

BAHAMA IS.

Mississippi R.

Belize

MOSQUITO COAST

JAMAICA

WEST INDIES

BARBADOS

Gibraltar

MINORCA

SENEGAL

St. Louis

Fort James

Whydah

Cape Coast Castle

ST. HELENA

BENGAL

CIRCARS

Bombay

Wandiwash

Pondicherry

Fort York (Bencoolen)

Britain and British possessions

0   500   1000   1500 miles

0   1000   2000 km

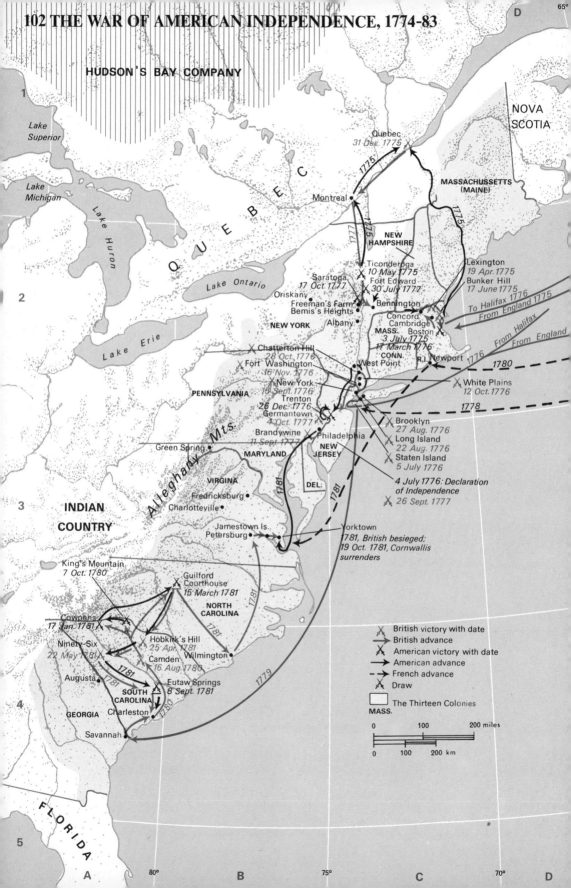

102 THE WAR OF AMERICAN INDEPENDENCE, 1774-83

HUDSON'S BAY COMPANY

NOVA
SCOTIA

*Lake
Superior*

*Lake
Michigan*

Lake Huron

Q U E B E C

MASSACHUSSETTS
(MAINE)

Quebec
31 Dec. 1775 ✕

Montreal

NEW
HAMPSHIRE

Lake Ontario

Lake Erie

Oriskany

Saratoga
17 Oct. 1777

Ticonderoga
10 May 1775
Fort Edward
30 July 1777

Freeman's Farm
Bemis's Heights

Bennington

Albany

NEW YORK

Lexington
19 Apr. 1775
Bunker Hill
17 June 1775

Concord
Cambridge
3 July 1775
Boston
17 March 1776

To Halifax 1776
From England 1775

MASS.

CONN.

Chatterton Hill
28 Oct. 1776

Fort Washington
16 Nov. 1776

West Point

R.I. Newport

From Halifax

New York
15 Sept. 1776

PENNSYLVANIA

Trenton
26 Dec. 1776
Germantown
4 Oct. 1777

Brandywine
11 Sept. 1777

Green Spring

Alleghany Mts.

MARYLAND

Philadelphia

NEW
JERSEY

White Plains
12 Oct. 1776

1780

From England

1778

Brooklyn
27 Aug. 1776
Long Island
22 Aug. 1776
Staten Island
5 July 1776

*4 July 1776: Declaration
of Independence*

✕ *26 Sept. 1777*

VIRGINIA

Fredericksburg

Charlotteville

DEL.

INDIAN

COUNTRY

Jamestown Is.
Petersburg

Yorktown
*1781, British besieged;
19 Oct. 1781, Cornwallis
surrenders*

King's Mountain
7 Oct. 1780

Guilford
Courthouse
15 March 1781

Cowpens
17 Jan. 1781

NORTH
CAROLINA

Ninety-Six
22 May 1781

Hobkirk's Hill
25 Apr. 1781

Camden
16 Aug. 1780

Wilmington

Augusta

Eutaw Springs
8 Sept. 1781

SOUTH
CAROLINA

GEORGIA

Charleston

1779

Savannah

FLORIDA

✕ British victory with date
✕→ British advance
✕ American victory with date
→ American advance
--→ French advance
✕ Draw

The Thirteen Colonies

MASS.

0   100   200 miles

0   100   200 km

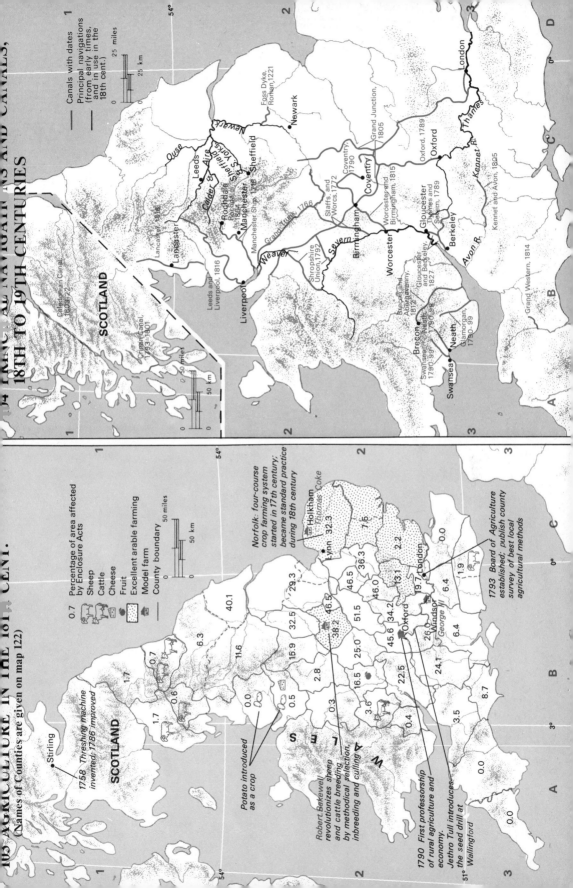

105 INDUSTRY AND COMMERCE IN THE 18TH CENT.
(For canals and navigations, see map 104)

Legend

- 10 ■ Chief town in 1801 with population in thousands
- 'Three cornered' slave trade
- Coal
- Ironworks
- Pottery
- Wool growing area
- Wool manufacturing centre
- Cotton
- Coastal shipping route
- *1764:* Coach time following improvement of roads (to London)
- Road

1776: 4 days
Glasgow 77
Edinburgh 82

1776: 3 days
Newcastle 28
Sunderland 12
Carlisle 10

Whitby

1774: 2 days
York 16
Hull 0

Preston
Bradford
Leeds 53
Halifax
Huddersfield 11
Bolton
Wigan 11
Bury
Manchester and Salford 84
Sheffield 31
Liverpool 78
Stockport 15
Lincoln 7

1781: 2 days
Chester 16
Burslem
Stoke
Derby 11
Nottingham 29

1764: 2 days
Shrewsbury 15
Broseley
Coalbrookdale
Bridgnorth
Bewdley
Birmingham 74
Coventry 16
Leicester 17
Lynn 10
Norwich 37
Yarmouth 15

Worcester 11
Cambridge 10
Ipswich 11
Colchester 14

Merthyr Tydfil
Swansea
Neath
Oxford 12

1779: 1-2 days
Bristol 64
Bath 32
Reading 10
Southwark 67
London 900
Chatham 11
Dover 15

Southampton 8
Portsmouth 32

Exeter 17

Plymouth 43

0   25   50
0   25   50 km

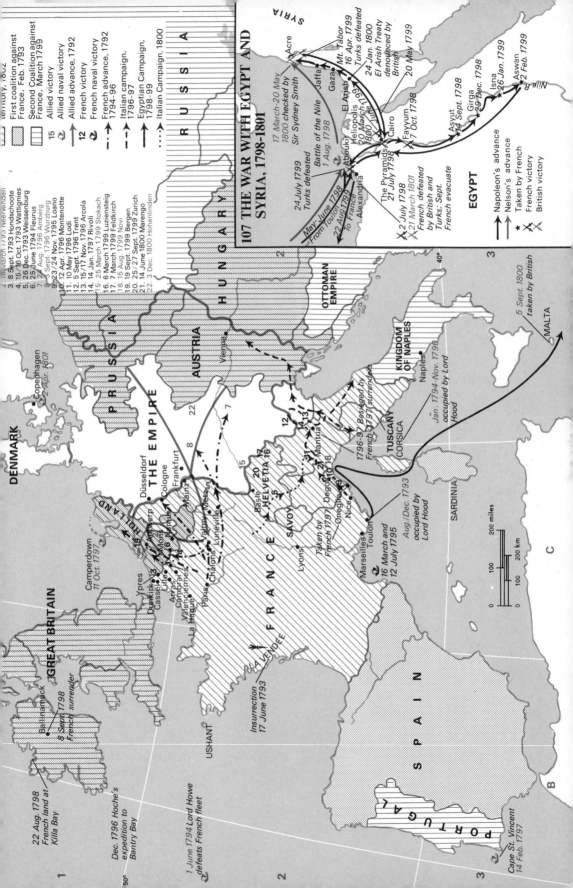

107 THE WAR WITH EGYPT AND SYRIA, 1798-1801

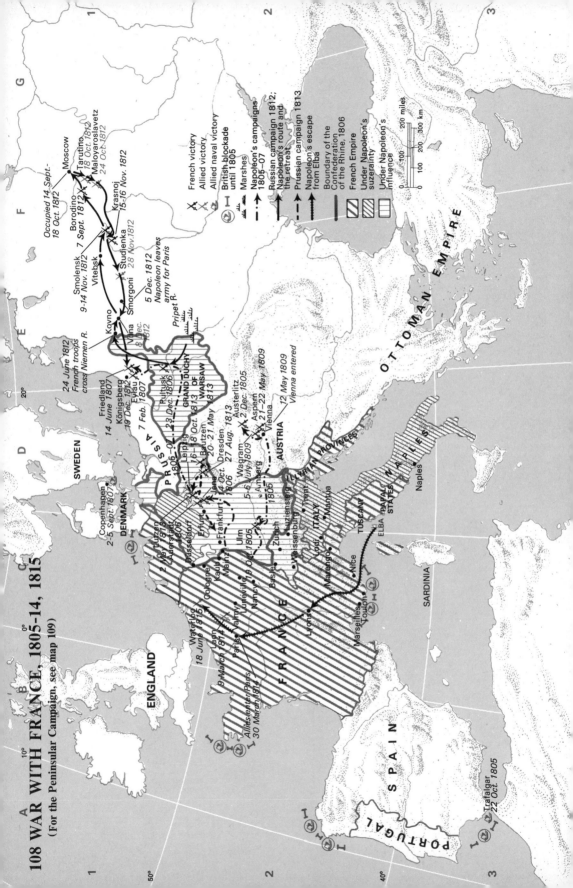

108 WAR WITH FRANCE, 1805-14, 1815
(For the Peninsular Campaign, see map 109)

Legend

- ✕ French victory
- ✕ Allied victory
- ⚓ Allied naval victory
- I British blockade until 1805
- ⫲ Marshes
- ·→·→· Napoleon's campaigns 1805-07
- ↑ Russian campaign 1812; Napoleon's route and the retreat
- ·↑·↑· Prussian campaign 1813
- ⇑ Napoleon's escape from Elba
- ▬ Boundary of the Confederation of the Rhine, 1806
- ▨ French Empire
- ▨ Under Napoleon's suzerainty
- ▥ Under Napoleon's influence

Scale: 0 100 200 miles / 0 100 200 300 km

Map labels

Moscow — Occupied 14 Sept.-18 Oct. 1812
Tarutino 18 Oct. 1812
Malojaroslavetz 24 Oct. 1812
Borodino 7 Sept. 1812
Krasnoj 15-16 Nov. 1812
Smolensk 9-14 Nov. 1812
Vitebsk
Studienka 28 Nov. 1812
Smorgoni 5 Dec. 1812 Napoleon leaves army for Paris
Kovno 8 Dec. 1812
Vilna
Pripet R.
24 June 1812 French troops cross Niemen R.
Friedland 14 June 1807
Königsberg
Eylau 7 Feb. 1807
Pultusk 26 Dec. 1806
GRAND DUCHY OF WARSAW 1813

SWEDEN
DENMARK
Copenhagen 2-5 Sept. 1807
P R U S S I A
Leipzig 16-18 Oct. 1813
1806-07
Lützen 2 May 1813
Auerstädt 1806
Bautzen 20-21 May 1813
Dresden 27 Aug. 1813
Erfurt
Düsseldorf
Cologne
Frankfurt 1806
Kaub
Mainz
Wagram 5-6 July 1809
Aspern 21-22 May 1809
Austerlitz 2 Dec. 1805
Vienna entered 12 May 1809
Amberg
AUSTRIA
Ulm 14 Oct. 1805
19 Oct. 1805
Weissenburg
Basel
Zürich
ILLYRIAN PROVINCES
Trent
Mantua
ITALY
Lodi
Milan
Marengo
TUSCANY
PAPAL STATES
NAPLES
Naples
ELBA
SARDINIA

ENGLAND
Waterloo 18 June 1815
Laon 9 March 1814
Allies enter Paris 30 March 1814
Paris
Valmy
Lunéville
Nancy
F R A N C E
Lyons
Nice
Marseilles
Toulon

S P A I N
PORTUGAL
Trafalgar 22 Oct. 1805

O T T O M A N   E M P I R E

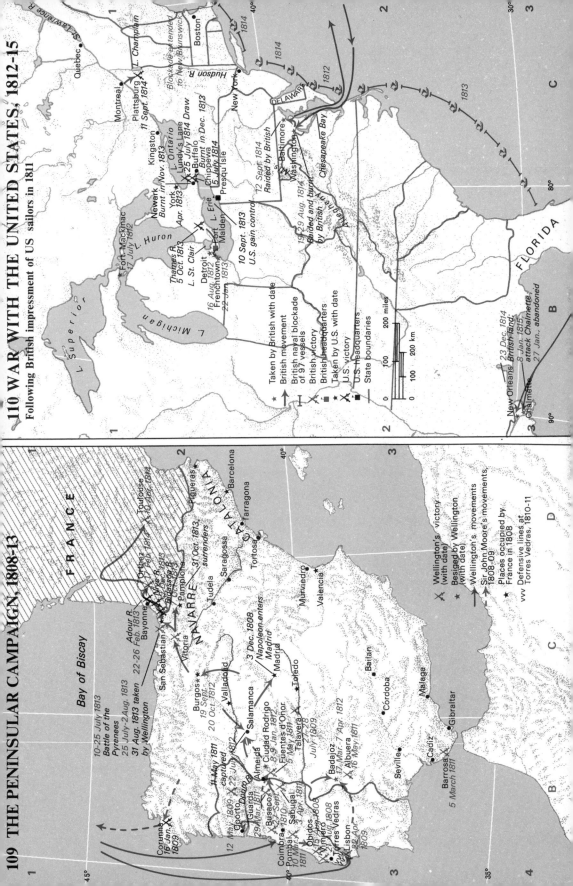

110 WAR WITH THE UNITED STATES, 1812-15
Following British impressment of US sailors in 1811

109 THE PENINSULAR CAMPAIGN, 1808-13

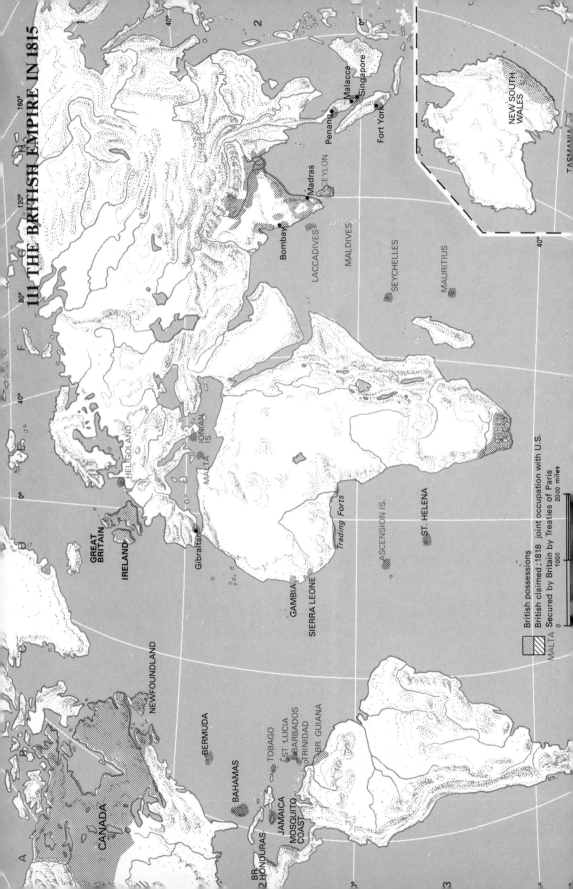

111 THE BRITISH EMPIRE IN 1815

NEW SOUTH WALES

TASMANIA

Malacca
Penang Singapore
Fort York

CEYLON
Madras

Bombay
LACCADIVES
MALDIVES

SEYCHELLES

MAURITIUS

GREAT
BRITAIN
IRELAND

HELIGOLAND
IONIAN IS.
MALTA
Gibraltar

GAMBIA
SIERRA LEONE

Trading Forts

ASCENSION IS.
ST. HELENA

British possessions
British claimed; 1818 joint occupation with U.S.
Secured by Britain by Treaties of Paris

MALTA

0   1000   2000 miles

CANADA

NEWFOUNDLAND

BERMUDA

BAHAMAS

TOBAGO
ST. LUCIA
BARBADOS
TRINIDAD
BR. GUIANA

JAMAICA
MOSQUITO
COAST
BR.
HONDURAS

112 RAILWAY EXPANSION IN THE 19TH CENT.
It is not possible to show all the branch lines on a map of this scale

Glasgow
Edinburgh
Ayr

Newcastle
Carlisle
Sunderland
Stockton
1825
Darlington
1825

Lancaster

Leeds
1811
Hull

Holyhead

Ruabon
Crewe
Lincoln

Norwich

Birmingham
Rugby
Cambridge

Colchester

Gloucester
Oxford

Merthyr Tydfil
1804 (experimental)
Cardiff
London

Bristol

Dover

Salisbury
Brighton

Exeter

Railways built before 1836
Railways built before 1845
Railways built before 1852
Railways built before 1914

Railway grouping 1921:
Southern
Western
North Western
North Eastern

0   25   50 miles
0   25   50 km

1830 Most trunk lines constructed
1836 1,000 miles completed
1840 1,331 m. completed
1840–50 'Railway mania'
1850 6,635 m. completed
1860 10,410 m. completed
1870 15,310 m. completed
1880 17,935 m. completed
1890 20,073 m. completed
1900 21,855 m. completed
1907 23,108 m. completed

54°
52°

1
2
3
4

A   4°   B   2°   C   D

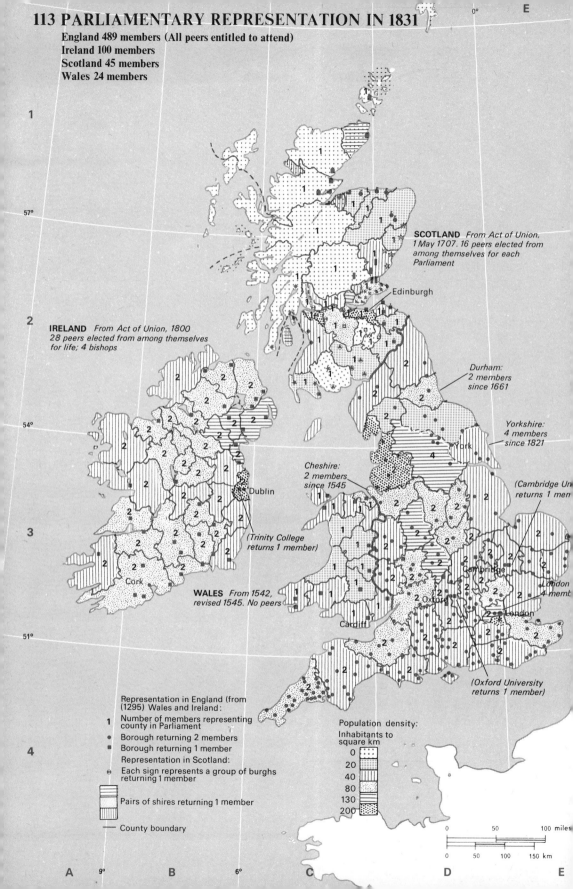

113 PARLIAMENTARY REPRESENTATION IN 1831

England 489 members (All peers entitled to attend)
Ireland 100 members
Scotland 45 members
Wales 24 members

SCOTLAND *From Act of Union,*
1 May 1707. 16 peers elected from
among themselves for each
Parliament

IRELAND *From Act of Union, 1800*
28 peers elected from among themselves
for life; 4 bishops

Edinburgh

Durham:
2 members
since 1661

Yorkshire:
4 members
since 1821

York

Cheshire:
2 members
since 1545

(Cambridge Un
returns 1 men

Dublin

(Trinity College
returns 1 member)

Cambridge

London
4 memb

Cork

WALES *From 1542,*
revised 1545. No peers

Oxford

London

Cardiff

(Oxford University
returns 1 member)

Representation in England (from
(1295) Wales and Ireland:

1   Number of members representing
county in Parliament

●   Borough returning 2 members

■   Borough returning 1 member

Representation in Scotland:

Each sign represents a group of burghs
returning 1 member

Pairs of shires returning 1 member

— County boundary

Population density:
Inhabitants to
square km
0
20
40
80
130
200

0   50   100 miles

0   50   100   150 km

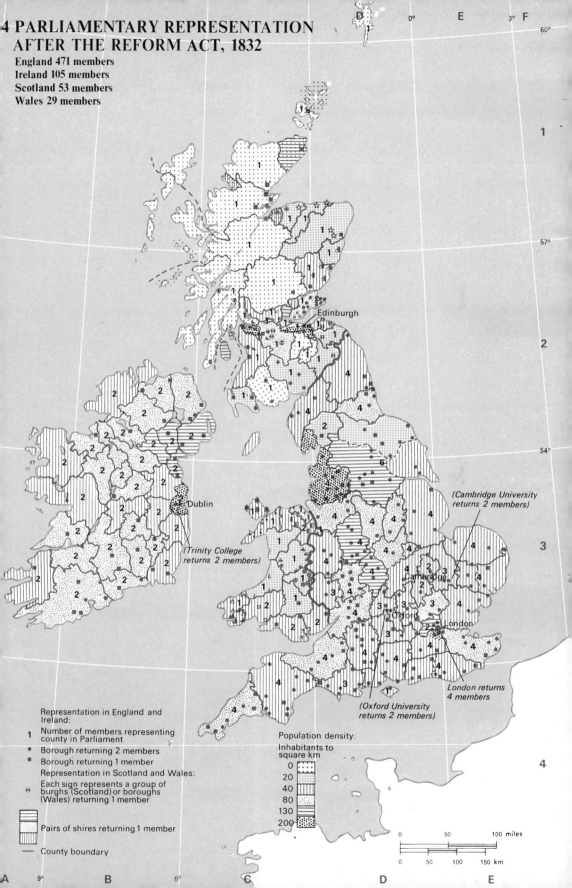

4 PARLIAMENTARY REPRESENTATION AFTER THE REFORM ACT, 1832

England 471 members
Ireland 105 members
Scotland 53 members
Wales 29 members

Edinburgh

Dublin

(Trinity College returns 2 members)

(Cambridge University returns 2 members)

6

Cambridge

Oxford

London

(Oxford University returns 2 members)

London returns 4 members

Representation in England and Ireland:

1   Number of members representing county in Parliament

●   Borough returning 2 members

■   Borough returning 1 member

Representation in Scotland and Wales:

Each sign represents a group of burghs (Scotland) or boroughs (Wales) returning 1 member

Pairs of shires returning 1 member

—   County boundary

Population density:
Inhabitants to square km

0
20
40
80
130
200

0   50   100 miles

0   50   100   150 km

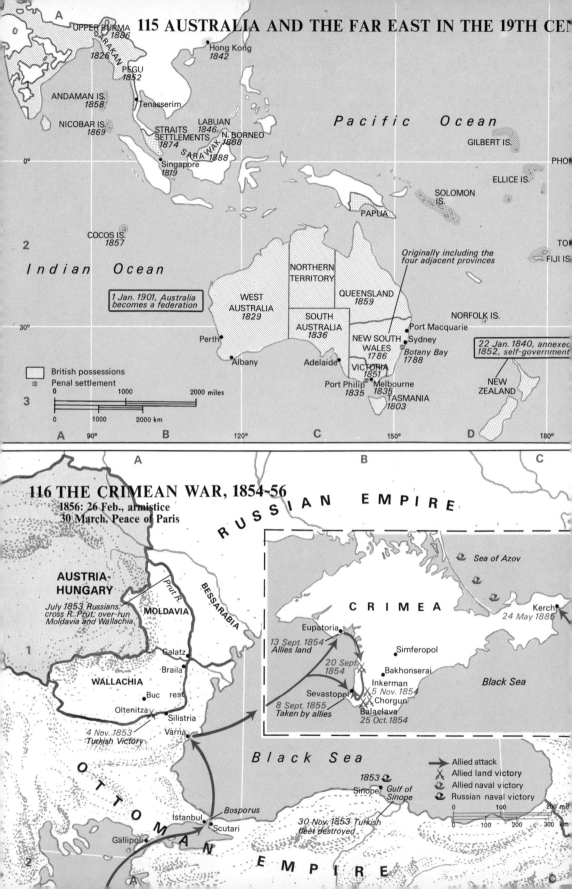

UPPER BURMA
1836

ARAKAN
1826

Hong Kong
1842

PEGU
1852

ANDAMAN IS.
1858

Tenasserim

Pacific Ocean

LABUAN
1846

N. BORNEO
1888

NICOBAR IS.
1869

STRAITS
SETTLEMENTS
1874

SARAWAK
1888

GILBERT IS.

Singapore
1819

PHO

0°

ELLICE IS.

SOLOMON
IS.

COCOS IS.
1857

2

PAPUA

*Originally including the
four adjacent provinces*

TO

FIJI IS

Indian Ocean

NORTHERN
TERRITORY

QUEENSLAND
1859

*1 Jan. 1901, Australia
becomes a federation*

WEST
AUSTRALIA
1829

NORFOLK IS.

30°

SOUTH
AUSTRALIA
1836

Port Macquarie

Perth

NEW SOUTH
WALES
1786

*Botany Bay
1788*

*22 Jan. 1840, annexec
1852, self-government*

Albany

Adelaide

VICTORIA
1851

◻ British possessions
⊞ Penal settlement

Port Philip
1835

Melbourne
1835

NEW
ZEALAND

0   1000   2000 miles

TASMANIA
1803

0   1000   2000 km

3

A   90°   B   120°   C   150°   D   180°

A   B   C

RUSSIAN   EMPIRE

**1856: 26 Feb., armistice
30 March, Peace of Paris**

Sea of Azov

AUSTRIA-
HUNGARY

Prut R.

BESSARABIA

CRIMEA

*July 1853 Russians
cross R. Prut; over-run
Moldavia and Wallachia*

MOLDAVIA

Kerch
24 May 1885

Eupatoria

1

Galatz

*13 Sept. 1854
Allies land*

Simferopol

Braila

*20 Sept.
1854*

Bakhonserai

WALLACHIA

Buc rest

Inkerman
5 Nov. 1854

Black Sea

Sevastopol

Oltenitza

*8 Sept. 1855
Taken by allies*

Chorgun

Silistria

Balaclava
25 Oct. 1854

*4 Nov. 1853
Turkish Victory*

Varna

OTTOMAN

Black   Sea

→ Allied attack
✕ Allied land victory
⚔ Allied naval victory
⚓ Russian naval victory

1853 ⚓

Sinope

*Gulf of
Sinope*

0   100   200 mil

Bosporus

0   100   200   300 km

İstanbul

Scutari

*30 Nov. 1853 Turkish
fleet destroyed*

Gallipoli

2

EMPIRE

A

140°   A   120°   B   100°   C   80°   D   60°   E   F

1

British Dominion
Annexed to Dominion
Dominion boundary
Canadian Pacific Railway
completed 7 Nov. 1886
Provincial boundary

0   250   500 miles
0   250   500 km

BRITISH COLUMBIA 1871, Joined Dominion

HUDSON'S BAY COMPANY
(Territory annexed to Dominion 1870)

Hudson Bay

Atlantic Ocean

60°

2

NEWFOUNDLAND

QUEBEC (Lower Canada)

Separately administered

Albany R.

St. Lawrence

QUEBEC
Quebec

NEW BRUNSWICK

U N I T E D   S T A T E S

L. Superior

Ottowa R.

ONTARIO (Upper Canada)

Montreal
Ottawa

NOVA SCOTIA

40°

L. Michigan

L. Huron

Toronto
Ontario
L. Erie   *L. Ontario*
Ontario

Prince Edward Island: joined Dominion 1873

3

A   B   120°   C   100°   D   80°   60°

A   70°   B   80°   C   90°   D   100°   E

1

KASHMIR
Peshawar

PUNJAB *1848*

Kumaon

Rohilkhand

T I B E T

BALUCHISTAN *1877*

Bikaner
Delhi

2

SIND *1843*

Ajmer

BHUTAN

ASSAM *1826*

RAJPUTANA

Benares
BIHAR

BENGAL *1765*
Dacca
Chandernagor *(French)*

BURMA *1886*

20°

Bundelkhand

Indore

CENTRAL PROVINCES *1861*

Gujarat
Diu (Portuguese)

Baroda

Nagpur
Berar

Calcutta

Mahrattas
Damão (Portuguese)

Bombay

NIZAM'S DOMINIONS

Hyderabad

Cuttack

Northern Circars

Pegu 1852

Rangoon

3

Goa (Portuguese)

Malabar

MYSORE

Konkan

Madras

Mahé (French)

Yanaon (French)

Pondicherry (French)

Karikal (French)

CEYLON

British possessions in 1763
British possessions acquired between 1763 and 1815
British possessions acquired between 1815 and 1856
Principal area of Indian Mutiny

0   200   400 miles
0   200   400   600 km

A   70°   B   80°   C   90°   D   100°   E

119 EXPANSION OF INDUSTRY IN THE 19TH CENTURY

For navigations and canals, see map 104, and railways, map 11.

BRITAIN IN SOUTH AFRICA IN THE 19TH CENT.

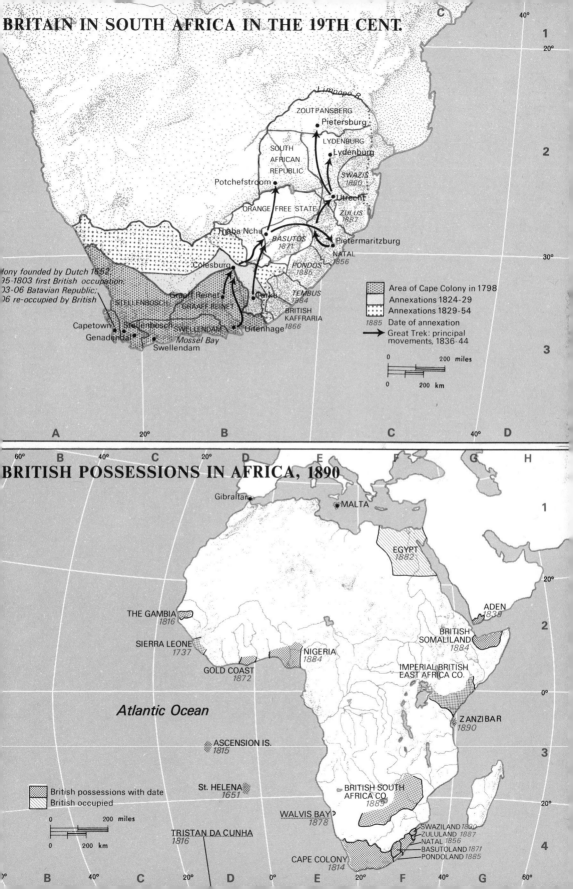

ZOUTPANSBERG

Limpopo R.

Pietersburg

LYDENBURG
Lydenburg

SOUTH
AFRICAN
REPUBLIC

SWAZIS
1890

Potchefstroom

ORANGE FREE STATE

Utrecht

ZULUS
1887

Thaba Nchu

BASUTOS
1871

Pietermaritzburg

Colesburg

PONDOS
1885

NATAL
1856

Graaff Reinet

GRAAFF REINET

Cradock

TEMBUS
1884

STELLENBOSCH

BRITISH
KAFFRARIA
1866

Capetown
Stellenbosch

SWELLENDAM

Uitenhage

Genadendal

Mossel Bay
Swellendam

olony founded by Dutch 1652.
95-1803 first British occupation.
03-06 Batavian Republic;
06 re-occupied by British

	Area of Cape Colony in 1798
	Annexations 1824-29
	Annexations 1829-54
1885	Date of annexation
→	Great Trek: principal movements, 1836-44

0   200 miles

0   200 km

BRITISH POSSESSIONS IN AFRICA, 1890

Gibraltar

MALTA

EGYPT
1882

THE GAMBIA
1816

ADEN
1839

SIERRA LEONE
1737

NIGERIA
1884

BRITISH
SOMALILAND
1884

GOLD COAST
1872

IMPERIAL BRITISH
EAST AFRICA CO.

Atlantic Ocean

ZANZIBAR
1890

ASCENSION IS.
1815

St. HELENA
1651

BRITISH SOUTH
AFRICA CO.
1889

WALVIS BAY
1878

	British possessions with date
	British occupied

SWAZILAND *1890*
ZULULAND *1887*
NATAL *1856*
BASUTOLAND *1871*
PONDOLAND *1885*

0   200 miles

0   200 km

TRISTAN DA CUNHA
1816

CAPE COLONY
1814

122 LOCAL GOVERNMENT REFORM, 1888-98

The Local Government Act, 1888, instituted
Urban and Rural Districts, which could
only be shown on a very large map.
The Welsh Counties are those of 1836.
Scottish and Irish Counties are those of
the Acts of Union of 1707 and 1802.

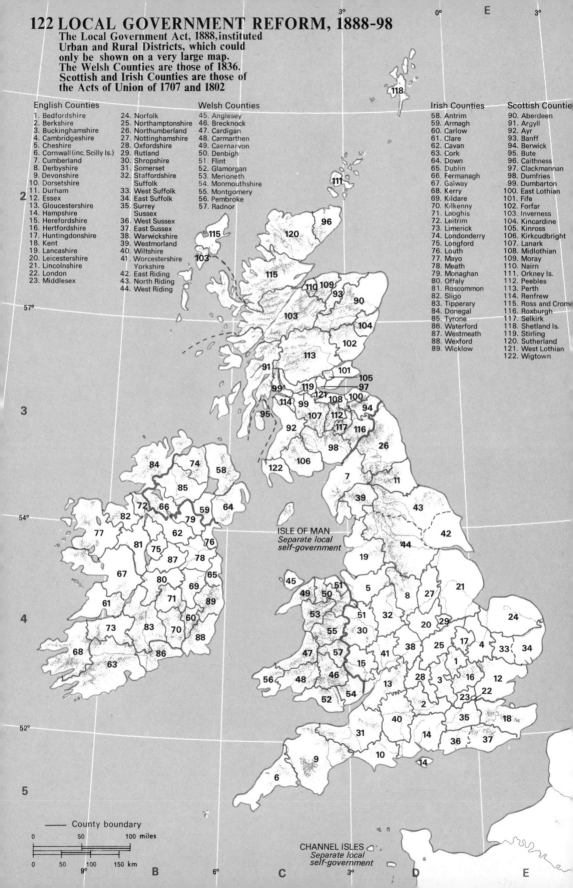

English Counties
1. Bedfordshire
2. Berkshire
3. Buckinghamshire
4. Cambridgeshire
5. Cheshire
6. Cornwall (inc. Scilly Is.)
7. Cumberland
8. Derbyshire
9. Devonshire
10. Dorsetshire
11. Durham
12. Essex
13. Gloucestershire
14. Hampshire
15. Herefordshire
16. Hertfordshire
17. Huntingdonshire
18. Kent
19. Lancashire
20. Leicestershire
21. Lincolnshire
22. London
23. Middlesex
24. Norfolk
25. Northamptonshire
26. Northumberland
27. Nottinghamshire
28. Oxfordshire
29. Rutland
30. Shropshire
31. Somerset
32. Staffordshire
    Suffolk
33. West Suffolk
34. East Suffolk
35. Surrey
    Sussex
36. West Sussex
37. East Sussex
38. Warwickshire
39. Westmorland
40. Wiltshire
41. Worcestershire
    Yorkshire
42. East Riding
43. North Riding
44. West Riding

Welsh Counties
45. Anglesey
46. Brecknock
47. Cardigan
48. Carmarthen
49. Caernarvon
50. Denbigh
51. Flint
52. Glamorgan
53. Merioneth
54. Monmouthshire
55. Montgomery
56. Pembroke
57. Radnor

Irish Counties
58. Antrim
59. Armagh
60. Carlow
61. Clare
62. Cavan
63. Cork
64. Down
65. Dublin
66. Fermanagh
67. Galway
68. Kerry
69. Kildare
70. Kilkenny
71. Laoghis
72. Leitrim
73. Limerick
74. Londonderry
75. Longford
76. Louth
77. Mayo
78. Meath
79. Monaghan
80. Offaly
81. Roscommon
82. Sligo
83. Tipperary
84. Donegal
85. Tyrone
86. Waterford
87. Westmeath
88. Wexford
89. Wicklow

Scottish Counties
90. Aberdeen
91. Argyll
92. Ayr
93. Banff
94. Berwick
95. Bute
96. Caithness
97. Clackmannan
98. Dumfries
99. Dumbarton
100. East Lothian
101. Fife
102. Forfar
103. Inverness
104. Kincardine
105. Kinross
106. Kirkcudbright
107. Lanark
108. Midlothian
109. Moray
110. Nairn
111. Orkney Is.
112. Peebles
113. Perth
114. Renfrew
115. Ross and Cromarty
116. Roxburgh
117. Selkirk
118. Shetland Is.
119. Stirling
120. Sutherland
121. West Lothian
122. Wigtown

ISLE OF MAN
*Separate local
self-government*

County boundary

0   50   100 miles

0   50   100   150 km

CHANNEL ISLES
*Separate local
self-government*

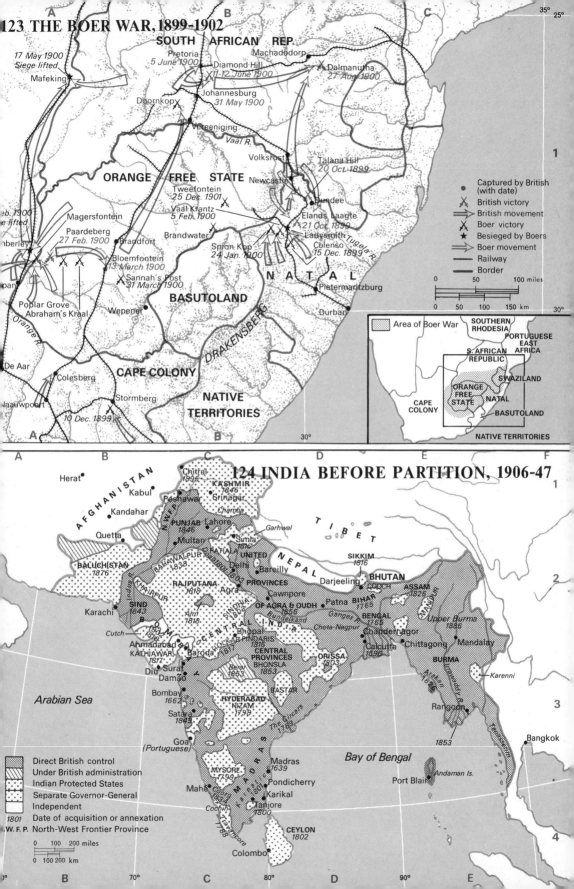

123 THE BOER WAR, 1899-1902

SOUTH AFRICAN REP.

17 May 1900
Siege lifted
Mafeking

Pretoria
5 June 1900
Machadodorp

Diamond Hill
X *11-12 June 1900*

Dalmanutha
27 Aug.1900

Doornkop

Johannesburg
31 May 1900

Vereeniging

Vaal R.

Volksrust

Talana Hill
20 Oct. 1899

ORANGE FREE STATE

Newcastle

Dundee

Tweefontein
25 Dec. 1901

Magersfontein

Vaal Krantz
5 Feb. 1900

Elands Laagte
21 Oct. 1899

eb. 1900
e lifted

Paardeberg
27 Feb. 1900

Brandfort

Brandwater

Ladysmith
15 Dec. 1899

Colenso
15 Dec. 1899

mberley

Bloemfontein
13 March 1900

Spion Kop
24 Jan. 1900

Tugela R.

pan

Sannah's Post
31 March 1900

N A T A L

Poplar Grove
Abraham's Kraal

Wepener

BASUTOLAND

Pietermaritzburg

Orange R.

De Aar

Colesberg

Stormberg

DRAKENSBERG

Durban

laauwpoort

CAPE COLONY

NATIVE
TERRITORIES

10 Dec. 1899

A   B   30°

Legend:
- • Captured by British (with date)
- ✕ British victory
- ⇉ British movement
- ✗ Boer victory
- ★ Besieged by Boers
- ⇉ Boer movement
- — Railway
- ━ Border

0   50   100 miles
0   50   100   150 km

Inset:
Area of Boer War

SOUTHERN RHODESIA

PORTUGUESE EAST AFRICA

S. AFRICAN REPUBLIC

SWAZILAND

ORANGE FREE STATE

NATAL

CAPE COLONY

BASUTOLAND

NATIVE TERRITORIES

---

124 INDIA BEFORE PARTITION, 1906-47

Herat

Chitral
1895

KASHMIR
1846

AFGHANISTAN

Kabul

Peshawar

Srinagar

Chamba

Kandahar

N.W.F.P.

PUNJAB
1846

Lahore

Garhwal

T I B E T

Quetta

Multan

Simla
1816

BALUCHISTAN
1876

BAHAWALPUR
1838

PATIALA

UNITED

Delhi

Bareilly

N E P A L

SIKKIM
1816

BHUTAN

Darjeeling

COOCH

ASSAM
1826

Karachi

SIND
1843

KHAIRPUR

RAJPUTANA
1818

SINDHIA
1803

Agra

PROVINCES

OF AGRA & OUDH
1856

Cawnpore

Patna

BIHAR

MANIPUR

Upper Burma
1886

Cutch

Amb.
1818

C E N T R A L   I N D I A

Bundelkand

BENGAL
1765

Chandernagor

Mandalay

Ahmadabad

KATHIAWAR
1817

Baroda

BHOPAL
1817

HOLKAR
1818

CENTRAL
PROVINCES

BHONSLA
1853

Chota Nagpur

Ganges R.

Calcutta
1690

Chittagong

BURMA

Diu

Surat

Damão

Berar
1853

ORISSA
1803

Karenni

Bombay
1662

BASTAR

Irrawaddy R.

Satara
1848

HYDERABAD
NIZAM
1799

Rangoon

Goa
(Portuguese)

The Circars
1788

1853

Bangkok

Madras
1639

Arabian Sea

MYSORE
1799

Pondicherry

Port Blair

Andaman Is.

Bay of Bengal

Mahé

M A D R A S

Karikal

Tenasserim

Cochin

Tanjore
1800

Travancore
1788

CEYLON
1802

Legend:
- Direct British control
- Under British administration
- Indian Protected States
- Separate Governor-General
- Independent

1801 Date of acquisition or annexation
.W.F.P. North-West Frontier Province

0   100   200 miles
0   100 200 km

Colombo

A   70°   B   C   80°   D   90°   E

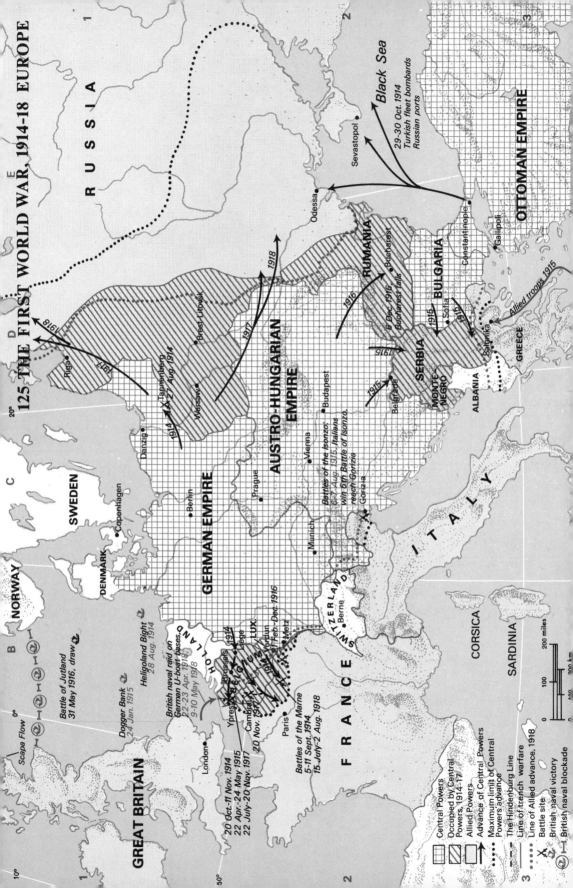

125 THE FIRST WORLD WAR, 1914-18 EUROPE

RUSSIA

NORWAY

SWEDEN

DENMARK

Copenhagen

GREAT BRITAIN

London

Scapa Flow

Battle of Jutland
31 May 1916, draw

Dogger Bank
24 Jan. 1915

Heligoland Bight
28 Aug. 1914

British naval raid on
German U-boat bases.
22-23 Apr. 1918
9-10 May 1918

HOLLAND

Danzig

Berlin

GERMAN EMPIRE

Brest-Litovsk

Tannenberg
27 Aug. 1914

Warsaw

1914

1918

1917

1917

1918

Riga

Odessa

1918

1916

1917

AUSTRO-HUNGARIAN
EMPIRE

Prague

Munich

Vienna

Budapest

RUMANIA

Bucharest
6 Dec. 1916
Bucharest falls

Sevastopol

Black Sea

29-30 Oct. 1914
Turkish fleet bombards
Russian ports

OTTOMAN EMPIRE

Constantinople

Gallipoli

BULGARIA

Sofia

1916

1915

1916

1915

SERBIA

Belgrade

1915

MONTE-
NEGRO

ALBANIA

Salonika

GREECE

Allied troops 1915

Battles of the Isonzo:
6-7 Aug. 1915, Italians
win 6th Battle of Isonzo,
reach Gorizia

Gorizia

ITALY

SWITZERLAND

Berne

Metz
Verdun
21 Feb.-Dec. 1916

Sedan

LUX.

Liège
1914

BELGIUM

Brussels
1914

Ypres

Cambrai
20 Nov. 1917

FRANCE

Paris

Battles of the Marne
5-11 Sept. 1914
15 July-2 Aug. 1918

20 Oct.-11 Nov. 1914
22 Apr.-24 May 1915
22 July-20 Nov. 1917

CORSICA

SARDINIA

50°

10°

0°

20°

Central Powers

Occupied by Central
Powers, 1914-17

Allied Powers

Advance of Central Powers

Maximum limit of Central
Powers' advance

The Hindenburg Line

Line of trench warfare

Line of Allied advance, 1918

Battle site

British naval victory

British naval blockade

0   100   200 miles

0   100   200 km

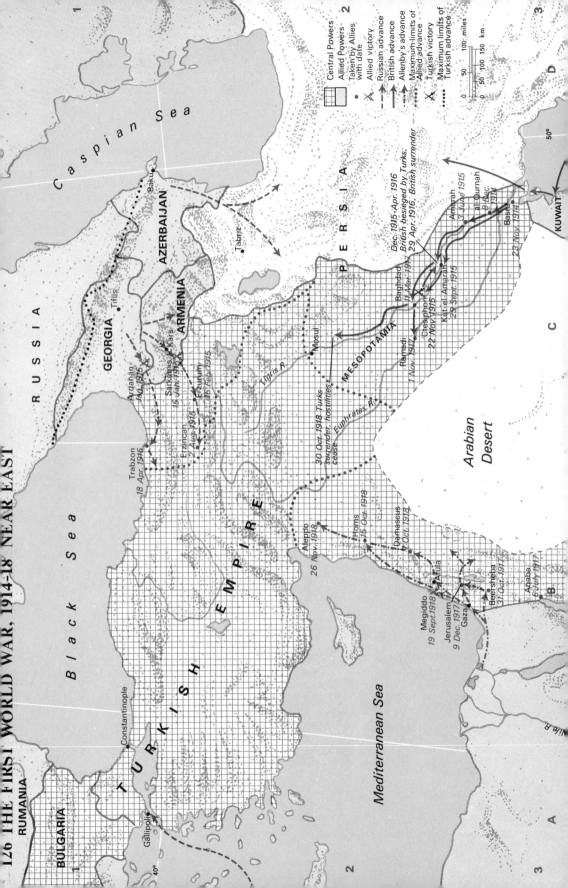

126 THE FIRST WORLD WAR, 1914–18: NEAR EAST

RUMANIA

BULGARIA

Black Sea

Caspian Sea

RUSSIA

Constantinople

Gallipoli

Baku

GEORGIA
Tiflis

AZERBAIJAN

ARMENIA
Kars

Tabriz

Ardahan
Jan. 1915

Sarikamis
15 Jan. 1915

Erzurum
16 Feb. 1915

Erzincan

Trabzon
18 Apr. 1916

2 Aug. 1916

T U R K I S H   E M P I R E

Tigris R.

Mosul

Euphrates R.

30 Oct. 1918 Turks
surrender, hostilities
cease

Mediterranean Sea

Aleppo
26 Nov. 1918

Homs

Damascus
1 Oct. 1918

Afula
Megiddo
19 Sept.1918

Jerusalem
9 Dec. 1917

Gaza

Beersheba
31 Oct. 1917

Aqaba
6 July 1917

*Arabian
Desert*

P E R S I A

M E S O P O T A M I A

Baghdad
11 Mar. 1917

Ctesiphon
22 Nov. 1915

Ramadi
1 Nov. 1917

Kut-el-Amarah
29 Sept. 1915

Dec. 1915–Apr. 1916
British besieged by Turks:
29 Apr. 1916, British surrender

Amarah
3 June 1915

al-Qurnah
8 Dec.
1914

Basra
23 Nov. 1914

KUWAIT

Nile R.

40°

50°

Central Powers
Allied Powers
Taken by Allies
with date
Allied victory
Russian advance
British advance
Allenby's advance
Maximum limits of
Allied advance
Turkish victory
Maximum limits of
Turkish advance

0   50   100   150   km
0   50   100   150   miles

127 THE PARTITION OF IRELAND, 1922

Following Government of Ireland Act,
1920 and treaty of 6 Dec. 1921.
First Northern Ireland Parliament met
5 June 1921; name of Irish Free State
agreed by Dail 7 Jan. 1922; became
Republic of Ireland 29 Dec. 1937

56°

C   6°   D

1

• Londonderry
LONDONDERRY

DONEGAL

ANTRIM

TYRONE

NORTHERN IRELAND
ULSTER

Belfast •

FERMANAGH

Armagh •

ARMAGH

MONAGHAN

Sligo •

L E I T R I M

SLIGO

CAVAN

LOUTH

54°

MAYO

Knock •

ROSCOMMON

Irish Sea

C O N N A U G H T

LONGFORD

MEATH

WESTMEATH

D U B L I N

GALWAY

IRISH FREE STATE

Maynooth •

• Dublin
(Kilmainham)

• Galway

OFFALY

KILDARE
The Curragh

L E I N S T E R   WICKLOW

2

LEIX

CLARE

• Ennis

CARLOW

KILKENNY

TIPPERARY

• Vinegar Hill

LIMERICK

WEXFORD

M U N S T E R

• Wexford
Rosslare •

KERRY

Waterford •

WATERFORD

52°

Killarney •

CORK

Cork •

━━━ Northern Ireland boundary
──── Provincial boundary
──── County boundary

0   20   40 miles

0   20   40   60 km

3

A   10°   B   8°   C   6°   D

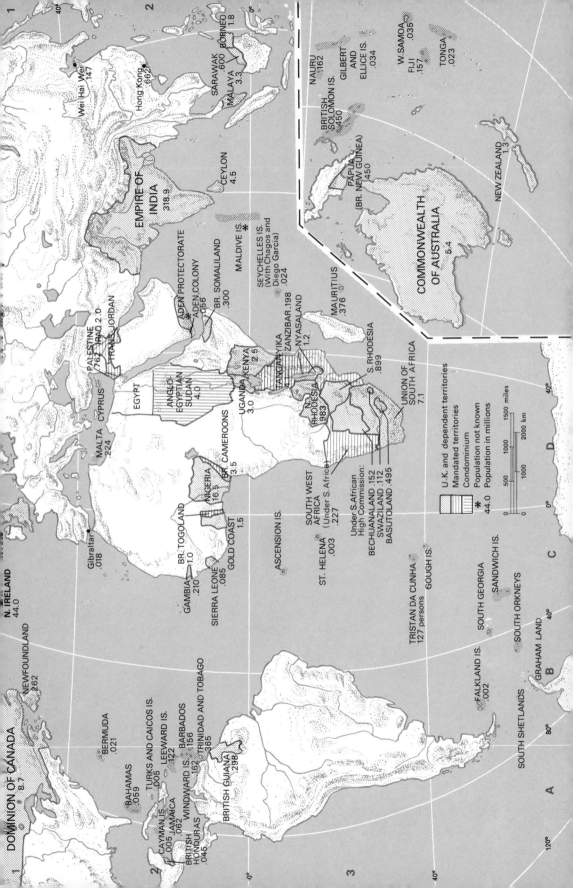

DOMINION OF CANADA
8.7

NEWFOUNDLAND
.262

N. IRELAND
44.0

Wei Hai Wei
.147

Hong Kong
.662

BORNEO
1.8

SARAWAK .600
MALAYA
3.3

NAURU
.162

GILBERT
AND
ELLICE IS.
.034

W.SAMOA
.035
FIJI
.157

TONGA
.023

BRITISH
SOLOMON IS.
.450

EMPIRE OF
INDIA
318.9

CEYLON
4.5

PAPUA
(BR. NEW GUINEA)
.450

NEW ZEALAND
1.3

ADEN PROTECTORATE

ADEN COLONY
.056

BR. SOMALILAND
.300

MALDIVE IS.
*

SEYCHELLES IS.
(With Chagos and
Diego Garcia)
.024

COMMONWEALTH
OF AUSTRALIA
5.4

MAURITIUS
.376

PALESTINE
.761 IRAQ 2.0
TRANS-JORDAN

CYPRUS
MALTA
.224

EGYPT

ANGLO-
EGYPTIAN
SUDAN
4.0

UGANDA
3.0

KENYA
2.5

TANGANYIKA
ZANZIBAR .198

NYASALAND
1.2

N.RHODESIA
.9833

S. RHODESIA
.899

UNION OF
SOUTH AFRICA
7.1

Gibraltar
.018

BR. CAMEROONS
3.5

NIGERIA
16.5

BR. TOGOLAND
1.0

GOLD COAST
1.5

SOUTH WEST
AFRICA
(Under S.Africa)
.227

Under S.African
High Commission:
BECHUANALAND .152
SWAZILAND .112
BASUTOLAND .495

GAMBIA
.210

SIERRA LEONE
.085

ASCENSION IS.

ST. HELENA
.003

TRISTAN DA CUNHA
127 persons

GOUGH IS.

U.K. and dependent territories
Mandated territories
Condominium
* Population not known
44.0 Population in millions

500   1000   1500 miles
0   1000   2000 km

BERMUDA
.021

BAHAMAS
.059

TURKS AND CAICOS IS.
.005

CAYMAN IS.
.005 JAMAICA
1.162

BRITISH
HONDURAS
.045

LEEWARD IS.
.322

WINDWARD IS.
.162

BARBADOS
.156

TRINIDAD AND TOBAGO
.365

BRITISH GUIANA
.298

FALKLAND IS.
.002

SOUTH GEORGIA

SANDWICH IS.

SOUTH ORKNEYS

SOUTH SHETLANDS

GRAHAM LAND

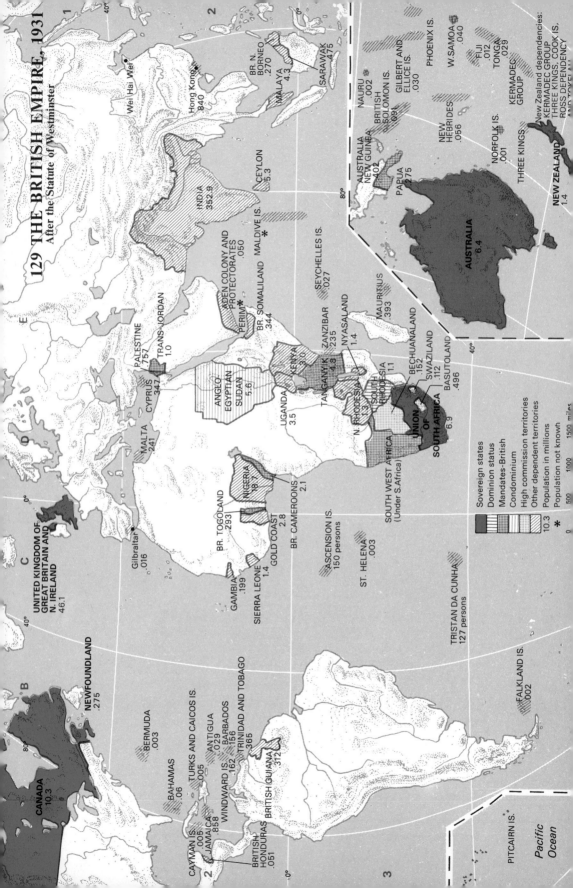

129 THE BRITISH EMPIRE, 1931
After the Statute of Westminster

UNITED KINGDOM OF GREAT BRITAIN AND N. IRELAND
46.1

CANADA
10.3

NEWFOUNDLAND
.275

BERMUDA
.003

BAHAMAS
.06

CAYMAN IS.
.005

JAMAICA
.858

TURKS AND CAICOS IS.
.005

BRITISH HONDURAS
.051

ANTIGUA
.029

BARBADOS
.156

WINDWARD IS.
.162

TRINIDAD AND TOBAGO
.365

BRITISH GUIANA
.312

FALKLAND IS.
.002

PITCAIRN IS.

Pacific Ocean

Gibraltar
.016

MALTA
.241

CYPRUS
.347

PALESTINE
.757

TRANS-JORDAN
1.0

ANGLO-EGYPTIAN SUDAN
5.6

ADEN COLONY AND PROTECTORATES
.050

PERIM *

BR. SOMALILAND
.344

MALDIVE IS.
*

CEYLON
5.3

INDIA
352.9

Wei Hai Wei

Hong Kong
.840

BR. N. BORNEO
.270

MALAYA
4.3

SARAWAK
.475

NAURU
.002

BRITISH SOLOMON IS.
.091

GILBERT AND ELLICE IS.
.030

PHOENIX IS.

W. SAMOA
.040

FIJI
.012

TONGA
.029

KERMADEC GROUP

AUSTRALIA NEW GUINEA
.402

NEW HEBRIDES
.056

PAPUA
.275

NORFOLK IS.
.001

THREE KINGS

AUSTRALIA
6.4

NEW ZEALAND
1.4

New Zealand dependencies:
KERMADEC GROUP
THREE KINGS, COOK IS.
ROSS DEPENDENCY
AND TOKELAU

SEYCHELLES IS.
.027

ZANZIBAR
.235

NYASALAND
1.4

MAURITIUS
.393

KENYA
3.0

TANGANYIKA
4.8

UGANDA
3.5

N. RHODESIA
1.3

SOUTH RHODESIA

BECHUANALAND
.152

SWAZILAND
.112

BASUTOLAND
.496

UNION OF SOUTH AFRICA
6.9

SOUTH WEST AFRICA
(Under S. Africa)

BR. TOGOLAND
.293

NIGERIA
18.7

GOLD COAST
2.8

BR. CAMEROONS
2.1

GAMBIA
.199

SIERRA LEONE
1.4

ASCENSION IS.
150 persons

ST. HELENA
.003

TRISTAN DA CUNHA
127 persons

Sovereign states
Dominion status
Mandates-British
Condominium
High commission territories
Other dependent territories
Population in millions
Population not known

10.3
*

0   500   1000   1500 miles

DEFEAT AND VICTORY IN EUROPE, 1939-40

England and the Allies
Allied movements
Russian movements following the Russo-German Pact 1939
Axis Powers, 1939
German advance
Occupied areas by 1940
German Border 1942
Maginot Line
German bombing missions

200 miles
100   300 km

UNION OF SOVIET SOCIALIST REPUBLICS

30 Nov. 1939 Russian invasion of Finland

March 1940 Area ceded to Soviet Union

10 Oct. 1939 Estonia, Latvia, Lithuania admit Soviet troops

17 Sept. 1939 Russian invasion of Poland

FINLAND

ESTONIA

LATVIA

LITHUANIA

SWEDEN

To Narvik

To Narvik

1940 Allied landings in Norway

9 Apr. 1940 German invasion of Norway and Denmark

Trondheim

Bergen
Oslo
Stavanger
Kristiansand

NORWAY

DENMARK
Copenhagen

EAST PRUSSIA

1 Sept. 1939 German invasion of Poland

Warsaw
Kutno
POLAND
Kielce
Modawa
Lvov

Berlin
GERMANY

BOHEMIA-MORAVIA
Prague

SLOVAKIA

AUSTRIA

HUNGARY
Budapest

RUMANIA
Bucharest

BULGARIA
Sofia

Belgrade
Sarajevo
YUGOSLAVIA

ALBANIA

GREECE

28 Oct. 1940 Unsuccessful Italian invasion of Greece

ITALY
Rome

Entered war 1940

CORSICA

SARDINIA

Black Sea

TURKEY

SPAIN
Madrid

PORTUGAL
Lisbon

Atlantic Ocean

GREAT BRITAIN
London

N. IRELAND

EIRE

May-June 1940 British invade Norway

28 June 1940 General de Gaulle recognized as head of French resistance

8 Aug.-5 Oct. Battle of Britain over southern England; R.A.F. defeats German Air Force

3 June 1940 Evacuated

Dunkirk
Amiens
Brussels
BELGIUM
Sedan
NETHERLANDS
Rotterdam
Wesermünde

Paris
Rennes
Tours

Dijon

Vichy

'Unoccupied France'

Munich

SWITZ.

Metz

10 May 1940

10 May-28 May 1940

10 May-26 June 1940 German invasion of France

Mainz

131 THE MIDDLE EASTERN THEATRE, 1939-43

SPAIN

PORTUGAL

40°

Tangier
Oran
Algiers
Bône
Bizerta
Tunis
MALTA
GREECE
TURKEY
CYPRUS
SYRIA 1941
IRAQ 1941
IRAN
Casablanca
12 May 1943 Germans surrender in North Africa
Tebessa
Gafsa
Sfax
Gabes
TUNISIA
Mareth Line
Tripoli
Gazala
D. rna
Benghazi
Tobruk
Bardia
Sidi Barrani
El Agheila
Agedabia
El Alamein
Cairo
Sept. 1943 Allied invasion of Italy
LEBANON 1941
Damascus
Baghdad
Habbaniyah
PALESTINE
TRANSJORDAN
Basra

MOROCCO
ALGERIA
LIBYA
EGYPT

S a h a r a   D e s e r t

FRENCH WEST AFRICA

ANGLO-EGYPTIAN SUDAN
ERITREA
YEMEN
17 March 1940 take Berbera
Aden
BRITISH SOMALILAND

BRITISH TOGOLAND

NIGERIA
FRENCH EQUATORIAL AFRICA

FRENCH SOMALILAND
Berbera
4-17 Aug. Taken by

GOLD COAST
FRENCH TOGOLAND
FRENCH CAMEROUN
BRITISH CAMEROONS

20 Jan. 1941 Emperor Haile Selassie restored; 5 Apr. Addis Ababa taken from Italians

Addis Ababa
ETHIOPIA
ITALIAN SOMALILAND
26 Feb. British, Mogadis
Mogad

BELGIAN CONGO
UGANDA
KENYA

0   500   1000 miles
0   500   1000 km
0°

Italy and annexed territory, 1940
British territory in Africa, 1940
VIIIth Army's advance, 1940-43
Ist Army's advance, 1942-43
German (Rommel) advance, 1941-42
1940 British takeover
Swamp area

132 THE FAR EASTERN THEATRE, 1941-45

ALASKA
CANA

U. S. S. R.

MONGOLIA
Aug. 1945
MANCHUKUO
Aug. 1945
Jehol
KURILE IS.
Aug. 1942 ATTU
ALEUTIAN IS.
KISKA
May 1942
Dutch Harbour
3 June 1942

CHINA
TIBET
NEPAL
INDIA

Hiroshima 6 Aug. 45
Nagasaki 9 Aug. 45
Shanghai
1 Apr.-2 July 1945
TAIWAN
OKINAWA
Tokyo
18 Apr. 1942
IWOJIMA 19 Feb.-16 Mar. 1945
MIDWAY
Battle of Midway 3-6 June 1942
UNI STA

HAWAII
Pearl Harbour 7 Dec. 1941

Hong Kong 8 Dec. 1941
INDO-CHINA
8 Dec. 1941
MARIANA IS.
SAIPAN
June 1944
GUAM
Battle of Philippine Sea 19 June 1944
ENINETOK
WAKE IS. 8 Dec. 1941
JOHNSTON
MARSHALL IS.
Jan. 1944

Rangoon
SIAM
Bangkok
ANDAMAN IS.
10 Dec. 1941
Manila
3 Mar. 1945
PHILIPPINES
Leyte Gulf 23-25 Oct. 1944
PALAU
TURK
Nov. 1943
GILBERT AND ELLICE IS.

BRUNEI
MOROTAI
Singapore
BORNEO
SUMATRA
Hollandia
NEW GUINEA
PAPUA
Rabaul
SOLOMON
Guadalcanal 7. Aug. 1942-7 Feb. 1943
Battle of Java Sea 27 Feb. 1942
JAVA
TIMOR
Port Darwin
Battle of Coral Sea 3-8 May 1942
NEW HEBRIDES
FIJI IS.
AUSTRALIA

Allies   Japanese
Territory held 194
Advance
Victory
Bombing mission
Atom Bomb atta
Maximum limit o Japanese conqu 1942

0   1000   2000 miles
0   1000   2000 km
100°
180°
140°

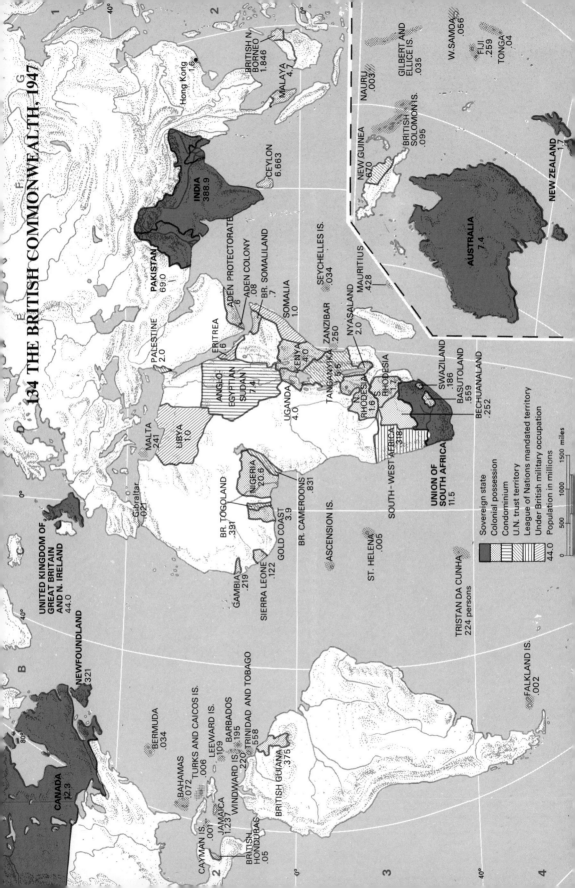

134 THE BRITISH COMMONWEALTH, 1947

UNITED KINGDOM OF GREAT BRITAIN AND N. IRELAND 44.0

NEWFOUNDLAND .321

CANADA 12.3

BERMUDA .034

BAHAMAS .072

TURKS AND CAICOS IS. .006

LEEWARD IS. .109

CAYMAN IS. .001

JAMAICA 1.237

BRITISH HONDURAS .05

WINDWARD IS. .220

BARBADOS .195

TRINIDAD AND TOBAGO .558

BRITISH GUIANA .375

FALKLAND IS. .002

TRISTAN DA CUNHA 224 persons

ST. HELENA .005

ASCENSION IS.

GOLD COAST 3.9

BR. TOGOLAND .391

GAMBIA .219

SIERRA LEONE .122

NIGERIA 20.6

BR. CAMEROONS .831

LIBYA 1.0

MALTA .241

Gibraltar .021

ANGLO-EGYPTIAN SUDAN 7.4

PALESTINE 2.0

ERITREA .6

ADEN PROTECTORATE .6

ADEN COLONY .08

BR. SOMALILAND .7

SOMALIA 1.0

UGANDA 4.0

KENYA 4.0

ZANZIBAR .250

SEYCHELLES IS. .034

NYASALAND 2.0

MAURITIUS .428

TANGANYIKA 5.5

N. RHODESIA 1.6

S. RHODESIA 1.7

SOUTH-WEST AFRICA .318

SWAZILAND .186

BASUTOLAND .559

BECHUANALAND .252

UNION OF SOUTH AFRICA 11.5

PAKISTAN 69.0

INDIA 388.9

CEYLON 6.663

Hong Kong 1.6

BRITISH N. BORNEO 1.846

MALAYA 4.7

NEW GUINEA .670

NAURU .003

BRITISH SOLOMON IS. .095

GILBERT AND ELLICE IS. .035

W. SAMOA .056

FIJI .259

TONGA .04

AUSTRALIA 7.4

NEW ZEALAND 1.7

Sovereign state
Colonial possession
Condominium
U.N. trust territory
League of Nations mandated territory
Under British military occupation
Population in millions

44.0

0 500 1000 1500 miles

35 BRITISH INDUSTRY IN THE 20TH CENT.

	Oil field
	Gas field
	Limit of Sector
	Oil pipeline
	Gas pipeline
	Proposed gas pipeline
	Oil refining
	Petrochemicals
	Chemicals
	Nuclear power station
	Hydro-electric station
	Shipbuilding
	Motor manufacture
	Iron and steel
	Coal
	Woollen manufacture
	Man-made fibre
	Fishing port
	Civil airport
	Carpets
	Linen
	Jute
	Cotton

MAGNUS
MURCHISON
THISTLE
TERN · DUNLIN
CORMORANT · STATFJORD
HEATHER · BRENT
LYELL · HUTTON
NINIAN
ALWYN

Lerwick

FRIGG

BERYL

CRAWFORD
NORWEGIAN

BRAE

PIPER · TONI
CLAYMORE · THELMA
TARTAN
MAUREEN
ANDREW

Kirkwall

Wick

Stornoway

BEATRICE

BUCHAN
FORTIES

MONTROSE

Peterhead
Cruden Bay
Aberdeen

LOMOND

EKOFISK

FULMAR
AUK
DANISH

ARGYLL

GERMAN

Dundee

BRITISH

Edinburgh

Glasgow

Firth of Clyde

DUTCH

Londonderry
Belfast

Newcastle

Teesport

Barrow-in-
-Furness

ISLE OF MAN

ROUGH · WEST SOLE
AMETHYST · VIKING
BROKEN BANK · INDEFATIGABLE
DEBORAH · S.E. INDEFATIGABLE
HEWETT · LEMAN BANK
DOTTIE
Bacton
Great-Yarmouth
Lowestoft

Dublin
Wylfa
Holyhead

Liverpool
Birkenhead
Manchester

Hull

Sheffield

Stoke-on-Trent

Nottingham

Whitegate

Birmingham

Gloucester

Sizewell
Ipswich

Luton

Milford Haven

Oxford
Coryton
London

Swansea
Cardiff · Bristol

Southampton
Bournemouth
Dungeness

Exeter

COREE
CASTLE

0   50 miles
0   50 km

St. Just
St. Mary's
SCILLY IS.

136 LABOUR RELATIONS, 19TH TO 20TH CENTURY
(For county boundaries see map 140)

Legend:
- Principal unemployment, 1920 – 39
- → The 'Hunger March' in 1936, down Great North Road
- *1920's* Strikes common (with date)
- Road

Scale: 0 — 50 — 100 miles / 0 — 50 — 100 — 150 km

SCOTLAND

Clydeside
1915, strikes

Stirling
Falkirk
Kirkcaldy
Dunfermline

Glasgow
Early 1930's

New Lanark
1820 ff. R. Owen's 'Model Mills'

NORTHUMBERLAND
1840 County Union formed
1844 Miners strike
1910 Miners strike

1874 Engineers strike successfully for 9 hour day

Early 1920's; late 1930's

Tyneside
1910 Railway strike; Boilermakers strike

Carlisle

Morpeth
Newcastle
Tyne
Consett
Durham
Jarrow
Sunderland
Hartlepool

1840 County Union formed
1844 Miners strike
1910 Miners strike

Workington
Whitehaven
Bishop Auckland
Teeside

YORKSHIRE
1840 County Union formed

1859 Weavers strike

Bradford
Burnley
Leeds

1831 First Trade Union formed
1839 Chartist Convention
1893 Miners strike-2 killed in riot

LANCASHIRE
1840 County Union founded
Preston and Stockport,
1853 47,000 spinners strike

Padiham
Preston
Huddersfield
Wakefield
Scunthorpe

1843 Miners' Association formed

1930's
Manchester
Barnsley
Rotherham
Sheffield

Accrington
1911 Weavers strike

1819 'Peterloo Massacre'
1826 'Old Mechanics' founded
1830 National Association for
Protection of Labour founded
1838 Chartist demonstration
1839 Anti-Corn Law League
founded
1899 General Federation of
Trades Union founded

Liverpool
1930's
Stockport

Stoke-on-Trent

1866 'Sheffield Outrages'

1911 Dockers' strike

Birmingham
1839 Chartist Convention

Coventry

NOTTINGHAMSHIRE
1811-1812 Luddites

WALES

STAFFORDSHIRE
1840 County Union forme

1901 Taff Vale Railway case

Llanelli
Merthyr Tydfil
Ebbw Vale
1893 Miners strike

Swansea
Port Talbot
Cardiff
Newport
Bristol
London

Tonypandy
1901 Miners strike and riot

1839 Riots
1920's

Southampton
1911 Dockers' strike becomes general

Tolpuddle
1834 'Martyrs' (pardoned 1836)

London:

1824-25 Combination Laws
1851 Amalgamated Society of Engineers founded
1852 First T.U. candidate stands in Parliamentary election
1859-60 Builders strike
1860 London Trades Council formed
1869 Trades Union Congress founded
1872 Factory Acts Reform Association founded. Abp. Manning supports Arch's Union
1874 10 working men stand at election
1885 First miner M.P.
1889 London Dock strike

1890 Hyde Park Meeting, 4 May
1906 Labour Party founded
1911 Suffragette violence at its peak. Dockers strike
1915 first Labour Ministers join Coalition
1918 57 Labour M.P.s elected
1918-19 London Police strikes
1922 142 Labour M.P.s elected
1923 191 Labour M.P.s elected
1924 Jan-Nov, Labour Government
1926 4 May-12 May, General strike;
1st May-19 Nov., Miners strike
1929 288 Labour M.P.s elected:
Labour Government to 1931
1940-45 Labour joins Coalition
1945-51 1964-70, 1973, Labour Governm

137 BRITISH UNIVERSITIES AND COPYRIGHT LIBRARIES, 1978

SCOTLAND

Aberdeen *1494*

Dundee *1967*
St. Andrew's *1410*
Stirling *1964*
Library of the Faculty of Advocates
Strathclyde *1964*
Edinburgh *1583*
Heriot–Watt *1966*
Glasgow *1451*

Coleraine *1968*
Ulster *1970*
NORTHERN IRELAND
Queen's Belfast *1845, 1909*

Newcastle upon Tyne *1963*
Durham *1832*

ENGLAND

Constituents of Queen's University:
Queen's, Belfast;
Queen's, Dublin;
Cork; Galway

Galway *1909*

Queen's *1845*
National Univ. *1909*
Dublin *1591*
Trinity College

EIRE

Cork *1909*

Lancaster *1964*
York *1963*
Bradford *1966*
Leeds *1904*
Hull *1954*
Salford *1967*
Liverpool *1903*
Manchester *1880*
Sheffield *1905*

Bangor
Keele *1962*
Nottingham *1948*
Loughborough *1966*
Leicester *1957*
East Anglia *1964*

University of Wales *1893*
Aberystwyth
WALES
Birmingham *1900*
Aston *1966*
Cambridge University Library
Cambridge (unknown)

National Library of Wales
Lampeter *1822*
Warwick *1964*
Buckingham *1976*
Open University *1969*
Essex *1964*

Swansea
Bodleian Library
Oxford (unknown)
British Museum

Cardiff
Bristol *1909*
Reading *1926*
Bath *1966*
Surrey *1966*
Kent *1965*

Southampton *1952*
Sussex *1961*

Exeter *1955*

London *1836*
Brunel *1966*
City *1966*

Leeds *1904* University with date of foundation
⬭ Copyright library

0   50   100 miles

0   50   100   150 km

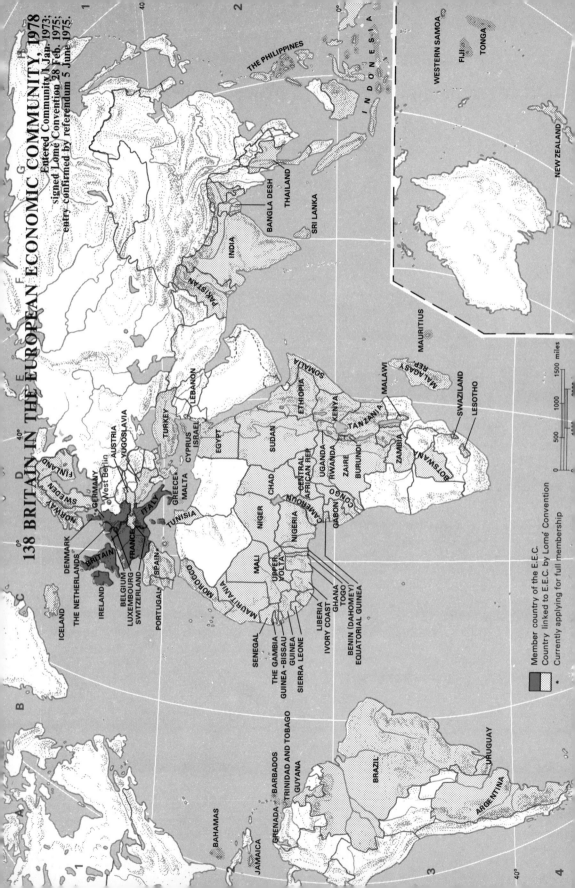

138 BRITAIN IN THE EUROPEAN ECONOMIC COMMUNITY, 1978

Entered Community 1 Jan. 1973;
signed Lomé Convention 28 Feb. 1975;
entry confirmed by referendum 5 June 1975.

Member country of the E.E.C.
Country linked to E.E.C. by Lomé Convention
* Currently applying for full membership

0   500   1000   1500 miles

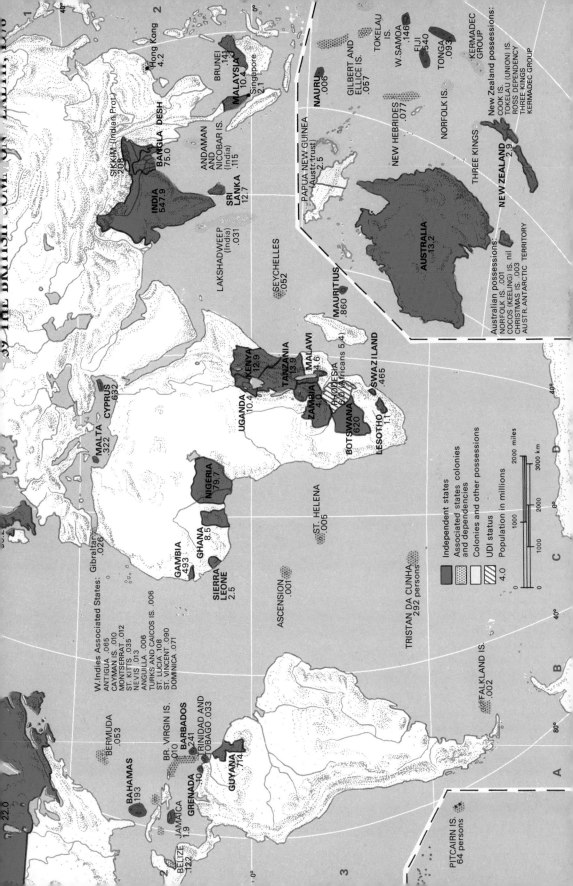

140 ENGLISH, SCOTTISH AND WELSH COUNTIES AND REGIONS, 1978

Following the Local Government Act, 1972,
and the Local Government (Scotland) Act, 1973

Scotland
Regions
1. Highland
2. Grampian
3. Tayside
4. Fife
5. Lothian
6. Borders
7. Central
8. Strathclyde
9. Dumfries & Galloway

Islands Areas
10. Orkney
11. Shetland
12. Western Is.

England
13. Greater London

Metropolitan Counties
14. Greater Manchester
15. Merseyside
16. South Yorkshire
17. Tyne & Wear
18. West Midlands
19. West Yorkshire

Non-metropolitan Counties
20. Avon
21. Bedfordshire
22. Berkshire
23. Buckinghamshire
24. Cambridgeshire
25. Cheshire
26. Cleveland
27. Cornwall
28. Cumbria
29. Derbyshire
30. Devon
31. Dorset
32. Durham
33. East Sussex
34. Essex
35. Gloucestershire
36. Hampshire
37. Hereford & Worcester
38. Hertfordshire
39. Humberside
40. Isle of Wight
41. Kent
42. Lancashire
43. Leicestershire
44. Lincolnshire
45. Norfolk
46. North Yorkshire
47. Northhamptonshire
48. Northumberland
49. Nottinghamshire
50. Oxfordshire
51. Salop
52. Somerset
53. Staffordshire
54. Suffolk
55. Surrey
56. Warwickshire
57. West Sussex
58. Wiltshire

Wales
59. Clwyd
60. Dyfed
61. Gwent
62. Gwynedd
63. Mid Glamorgan
64. Powys
65. South Glamorgan
66. West Glamorgan

—— New boundary
—— Old boundary

0   50   100 miles

0   50   100   150 km

This index has been made as concise as possible, and certain maps have not been indexed. Maps 1 and 2 are treated as simply pictorial. Scottish burghs listed in maps 69 and 95, Irish counties shown on map 127, English and Welsh counties in map 122, the new county boundaries in England, Wales and Scotland 1972 and 1973, and the names of oilfields which appear on map 135 have not been indexed because they can be found quite simply from those maps, most of which also have lists. Towns and cities whose names occur very frequently have been marked with an asterisk, and only the first incidence is shown, except where the town or city has a Latin name of Roman times, in which case two entries are shown.

INDEX